The United States Constitution

A History

Elgin L. Hushbeck, Jr.

Eudokia Enrichment Library
Book #1

Energion Publications
Gonzalez, Florida
2022

ISBN: 978-1-63199-827-0
eISBN: 978-1-63199-828-7
Kindle Textbook ISBN: 978-1-63199-837-9

Eudokia Enrichment Library
P. O. Box 841
Gonzalez, Florida 32560
The Eudokia Enrichment Library is an imprint of Energion Publications.

eudokialibrary.com
pubs@energion.com

Acknowledgments

First and foremost, I want to thank my wife, who is my friend and my partner. She has been an invaluable support and, at times, a sounding board for ideas. I could not do this without her. I also want to thank the many students I have had for their input and challenges, as they have helped me think through these issues. I also want to thank the numerous people I have talked with over the years about politics and the Constitution, particularly those who disagreed with me. As with some of my earlier books, Helen Wisniewski played an important role in reading and editing this book's early drafts. I want to thank my friends at Energion; my editor Chris Eyre for his valuable suggestions. This is a better book for his input. Finally, I want to thank my publisher Henry Neufeld for his kind support and encouragement.

Table of Contents

Introduction

While there are many ways to approach this subject, the main approach here will be historical. This approach allows for the introduction of concepts and controversies as they arose. It also allows for a better understanding of the Constitution's major schools of thought, their foundations, formations, the forces driving them, and the differences between them. Hopefully, this approach will make it easier to understand the different views existing today. I also hope that this understanding will foster better communication and reduced polarization.

After briefly setting the stage for the revolution, we will take the founding fathers, who created the constitutional government we have as our starting point. To keep things simple, herein, they and their latter advocates are called federalists. In this book, the major contrast will be between the federalists and the two major groups who disagreed with them. The first group were the supporters of slavery in the early 19th century. Since the beginning of the 20th century, the second has been the progressives and their intellectual descendants. At different times, these perspectives had other names. For example, progressives became liberals and now might be returning to the name progressive.

At the time of the revolution, the founding fathers would have been considered radicals. Then they became the founders. Today their followers are generally called conservatives. Still, both federalists and progressives have existed in both political parties, sometimes simultaneously.

What follows is a summary. Neither of these movements was by any means monolithic. Both the federalists and progressives contained a wide range of diversity and disagreement; each has differing schools of thought, and each has changed over time. The federalists were not all of one mind, and neither were progressives. Individuals themselves changed their views over time. Therefore, it would be a mistake to assume today's progressives are identical to those at the beginning of the 20th century. It would likewise be a mistake to assume the federalists' modern defenders agree with everything the founders did.

It is also important to point out that these two groups represent large political movements with concerns beyond the Constitution. When used in this book, these terms represent the major or core aspects of these views, particularly those aspects and teachings that impact the understanding of the Constitution and how government operates. The focus here is constitutional rather than political. Rather than carefully documenting all the various name changes, they are simply referred to as federalists and progressives.

As for the starting and ending dates, they are only rough guidelines. After all, while the Declaration of Independence will be our starting point, the document's roots go back much further, as do the revolution's roots. Likewise, progressivism did not spring into existence in 1901. Its roots go back further to another revolution, the French revolution, with major development during the latter part of the 19th century.

I have, as much as possible, used sources readily available on the internet. I have also tried to let the various people speak for themselves, and thus quotes in the book are more numerous and longer than might normally be found in a book of this size. Of course, I encourage people to read the sources in full, as there is no way to present their complete arguments and rationale in the limited space here. Finally, I have updated the spelling in direct quotes to conform to modern usage in a few places.

The Stage Is Set (Pre-1776)

The United States has the unique distinction of being one of the youngest countries, yet the oldest government in the world. While many countries like China and France have been around a lot longer, they have all had major changes in their system of government. France had its own revolution shortly after the American Revolution. China's communist government came to power in 1949.

Historical events don't just happen. They are a mixture of trends and choices, causes and effects operating within a historical framework. So one question is, why 1776? What led to the formation of the United States of America with its particular government at that particular time?

Historically, the British colonies started as settlements, the earliest to succeed being Jamestown in 1607. The settlements grew and became colonies, the last being Georgia in 1752. For the most part, the colonies were left alone to fend for themselves, with little oversight from the mother country. Since they needed some sort of government, each colony had its own based on their circumstances and the thinking of the period. By the time of the revolution, there were thirteen colonies, each with its own government. The oldest of these had well over a hundred years of experience in self-government.

Jamestown

The colonial governments had been influenced by the intellectual thought of the period, which was basically enlightenment ideas as refined by philosophers John Locke and Montesquieu. Their views centered around the rights of the individual. Locke wrote of the right to life, liberty, and property. The Declaration of Independence would change the latter to the pursuit of happiness when it borrowed the phrase.

Another major influence was the Great Awakening in the 1730s and 1740s. The Great Awakening was a time of both spiritual renewal and discussion. It spawned a great interest in education, which led to the founding of schools and colleges. It combined the enlightenment principles of reason with an emotional experience. As a movement that swept through all the colonies, it was the first step in creating an American experience. As historian Paul Johnson summed up the origins of the revolution,

> It was the marriage between the rationalism of the
> American elites touched by the Enlightenment with the
> spirit of the Great Awakening among the masses which
> enabled the popular enthusiasm thus aroused to be
> channeled into the political aims of the Revolution.[1]

All that remained was the spark. As the British colonies continued to grow and expand, they eventually ran into conflict with the French colonies in what is now Canada. Starting as a series of skirmishes in the Great Lakes area in which a young George Washington played an important role, the conflict eventually escalated

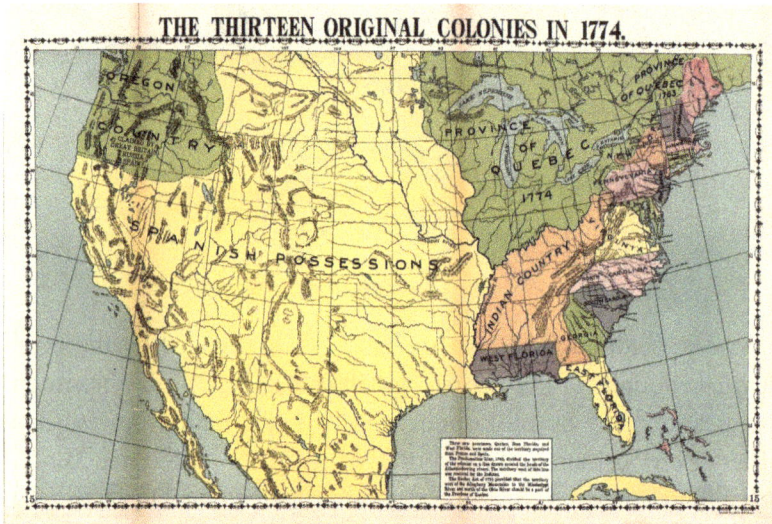

THE THIRTEEN ORIGINAL COLONIES IN 1774.

into the global Seven Years war. When it was over in 1763, Britain had won but was massively in debt.

From Britain's point of view, the colonies had dragged them into a costly war, leaving them with huge debts. To make matters worse, because they had largely been left to get on by themselves until that point, they did not pay as much in taxes as the average person in Britain, even though they were, on average, more prosperous. Many in the British government believed they had ig-

1   P. Johnson, *A History of the Ameican People*, New York: HarperCollin ,
1997, p 116

nored the colonies for too long. It was time to bring some order and control to the situation. A major part of this was that the colonies should pay more taxes to help cover the costs of the war fought on their behalf. The colonies, that had grown used to self-government and low taxes, had a different view of things.

When the colonies pushed back on the new restrictions and taxes, the British government doubled down on its efforts. Tensions flared with the Boston Massacre in 1770 and the Boston Tea Party in late 1773. On April 19, 1775, 700 British troops, sent to confiscate guns, encountered 77 colonists who gathered to resist

The Boston Massacre

the troops. No one knows who fired the "shot heard 'round the world'" but open conflict had begun.

Three weeks later, on May 10, the Second Continental Congress convened. By June, they established an army led by Washington.

In July, they sent a petition to King George seeking to end the conflict. In some respects, this was an attempt to circumvent Parliament by going directly to the King. It did not work. The King refused to read it, declaring the colonists were traitors. The chances for reconciliation were gone. Later that year, Congress established the Navy and the Marines. In January 1776, Thomas Paine anonymously published *Common Sense*, calling for independence from Great Britain, thereby bringing the question to the debate's forefront.

The Founding Era: Words Become Structure (1776-1801)

The Declaration of Independence

Like golden apples set in silver is a word spoken at the right time. Proverbs 25:11

Referring to Proverbs in a fragment of his writings on the Constitution, Abraham Lincoln wrote of the Declaration of Independence's principles; they were words spoken at the right time. He went on to say,

> The Union, and the Constitution, are the picture of silver, subsequently framed around it. The picture was made, not to conceal, or destroy the apple; but to adorn, and preserve it. The picture was made for the apple—not the apple for the picture.[2]

Here we come to the first of many points of controversy surrounding the Constitution. Is understanding the Declaration important for understanding the Constitution, or did the Constitution supersede the Declaration rendering it merely of historical interest but with little or no bearing on it? Lincoln's view was clear. The Constitution was not made to "conceal or destroy" the Decla-

2   A. Lincoln, "Fragment on the Constitution and Union," [Online]. Available: https://teachingamericanhistory.org/library/document/fragment-on-the-constitution-and-union/

13

ration but to "adorn and preserve it." Chief Justice Warren Burger expressed a similar view when he said, "The Declaration of Independence was the promise; the Constitution was the fulfillment." We will take up the criticisms of the Declaration as people raised them.

While it is difficult for us to understand now, try to put yourself into the mindset of a delegate to the Continental Congress in June 1776. They were representatives from thirteen separate colo-

Signing the Declaration of Independence

nies, each with its own government interests and concerns. They were closer to thirteen countries than a single nation. They were facing the strongest country on earth at the time, and now the King had branded them traitors. They had come together to work out a solution, and now people were openly discussing independence.

In June, the question of independence came up in Congress. Yet, colonies breaking away from the mother country had never happened before. This was something new. How would the colonies separate from Great Britain? They needed a statement of separation. Congress appointed a committee of five, which quickly realized Jefferson should produce the first draft. Years later, Jefferson would write,

> When forced, therefore, to resort to arms for redress, an appeal to the tribunal of the world was deemed proper for our justification. This was the object of the Declaration of Independence. Not to find out new principles, or new arguments, never before thought of, not merely to say things which had never been said before; but to place before mankind the common sense of the subject, in terms so plain and firm as to command their assent, and to justify ourselves in the independent stand we are compelled to take.[3]

This reasoning is made clear in the first paragraph, setting forth the purpose of the document.

> When in the Course of human events, it becomes necessary for one people to dissolve the political bands which have connected them with another, and to assume among the powers of the earth, the separate and equal station to which the Laws of Nature and of Nature's God entitle them, a decent respect to the opinions of mankind requires that they should declare the causes which impel them to the separation.

Having established its purpose, the Declaration then proceeded with a logical argument for independence, and as such, the second paragraph states the premises for that argument,

> We hold these truths to be self-evident, that all men are created equal, that they are endowed by their Creator with certain unalienable Rights, that among these are Life, Liberty and the pursuit of Happiness.--That to secure these rights, Governments are instituted among Men, deriving their just powers from the consent of the governed, --That whenever any Form of Government becomes destructive of these ends, it is the Right of the People to alter or to abolish it, and to institute new government,

3   Edited by the Hillsdale College Politics Faculty, *The U.S. Constitution: A Reader*, Hillsdale, Michigan: Hillsdale College Press. Kindle Edition., 2012. P. 11

These are the fundamental premises of the American government. People have rights given by God; the purpose of government is to protect those rights; ultimate political power rests with the people and, by inference, not with the King.

After some discussion of when it is proper to institute a new government, the Declaration lists some of the "injuries and usurpations" as "Facts… submitted to a candid world." After citing the attempts to work with the King and the people of Britain, the final paragraph says,

> We, therefore, the Representatives of the united States of America, in General Congress… and by Authority of the good People of these Colonies, solemnly publish and declare, That these United Colonies are, and of Right ought to be Free and Independent States; that they are Absolved from all Allegiance to the British Crown.

Before signing, the delegates included a pledge,

> And for the support of this Declaration, with a firm reliance on the protection of divine Providence, we mutually pledge to each other our Lives, our Fortunes and our sacred Honor.

This was no throwaway line. By signing this document, the delegates were making themselves marked men. They would be rounded up, killed, and their property confiscated should the effort for independence fail. Still, the war was won, and independence was secured with the surrender of General Cornwallis at Yorktown, October 17, 1781. Earlier that year, with the ratification of the Articles of Confederation, the Continental Congress became the Congress of the Confederation.

Articles of Confederation

It did not take long for problems with the Articles to become apparent. Even before the war was over, Hamilton began calling for a convention to fix the Articles and continued to do so until it was finally called. The core problem was a tension that continues to the present day. On one side is liberty, and the other is an effective government. Some government was needed. But every law passed by the government is a restriction on liberty.

The colonies were in the middle of a war for independence when the Articles were written. It is not surprising the government they created was too weak to do what needed to be done. As the 1780s progressed, discussions on how to fix the Articles grew.

Following the War, with hard currency in short supply, a debt crisis swept through the colonies. Soldiers returning home faced demands to pay their debts while they went unpaid by the Congress of the Confederation. Why were they unpaid? The reason was simple: Congress did not have any money to pay them and had little power to get it. One anecdote demonstrates the situation. When a messenger arrived with news of Cornwallis' surrender, Congress could not pay him. Members needed to chip in to cover his expenses.[4] Congress was completely at the mercy of the states, but the states had their own problems.

In 1786, the growing debt problems spawned Shay's Rebellion. Any expectations the federal government would put down the rebellion were dashed. Congress did not have enough money to pay soldiers from the Revolutionary War, much less raise funds for a new army. Eventually, the rebellion was stopped by an army raised by the Massachusetts state government. Still, a consensus was growing that something had to be done or the Union would simply fall apart.

The Constitution

The Convention

Finally, to Hamilton's relief, a convention was called to revise the Articles. Scheduled to start on May 14, 1787, it was not until May 25 that the Convention had the minimum number of seven states required to conduct business. All eventually sent delegates except Rhode Island, who refused to attend at all. Rhode Island

---

4   C. D. Bowen, *Miracle at Philadelphia*, New York: Little, Brown and Company, 1966, p 5

was concerned about the Convention being dominated by the larger states.

The delegates did three key things when the Convention got underway. First, they elected George Washington president, which

James Madison

greatly increased the Convention's stature and thus the stature of their result. Voting in the Convention was done by state, the same as under the Articles of Confederation. The delegates from a state would get together to determine how the state would cast its one vote on a given issue. Second, they went into a committee of the whole for most of their business. This allowed states to cast votes "in committee" that would not be binding, making it much easier for delegates to take provisional positions, which they could re-

18

consider and even change later. This happened many times and thus avoided the problems of people getting locked into votes. Finally, they made the proceedings secret, which greatly limited pressure from outside interests.

The Constitutional Convention

In addition to these decisions, the Convention had another advantage allowing it to succeed. Either by chance or design, they focused much more on practical matters than theory. While they were very well read in political theory and history, experience was also on their side. In many areas of life, the first attempt at something is rarely the best, and the Articles had failed, and the reasons for the failure were apparent. In addition, the delegates were deeply involved in their state governments. So while they understood the theory, they brought a lot of practical knowledge regarding what worked and what did not from their time in state government and the failure of the Articles. As John Dickinson from Delaware put it, "experience must be our only guide. Reason may mislead us."[5]

5   J. Willson, "A Look at One of Our Lost Founders," 1 August 2010. [Online]. Available: https://theimaginativeconservative.org/2010/08/willson-lost-founder-john-dickinson.html. [Accessed 3 September 2020]

A fundamental problem that faced the delegates was the same that doomed the Articles. How to create a government that lives up to the Declaration's principles, one strong enough to secure the people's rights, and yet not so strong that it, itself, tramples those rights. Madison summed up the problem in a famous quote from Federalist #51,

> But what is government itself but the greatest of all reflections on human nature? If men were angels, no government would be necessary. If angels were to govern men, neither external nor internal controls on government would be necessary. In framing a government which is to be administered by men over men, the great difficulty lies in this: You must first enable the government to control the governed; and in the next place, oblige it to control itself.

Human nature was not all bad for the federalists but had traits such as greed and ambition that could threaten liberty. These needed to be overcome. This concept of human nature will become another point of controversy in the future. Nor was this simply restricted to the government. As Madison went on to say in Federalist #51,

> It is of great importance in a republic, not only to guard the society against the oppression of its rulers; but to guard one part of the society against the injustice of the other part. Different interests necessarily exist in different classes of citizens. If a majority be united by a common interest, the rights of the minority will be insecure.

A key question in any democratic form of government is how are decisions to be made? A simple and democratic solution is fifty percent plus one. Whichever side has the most votes wins. While a common solution, it does have a problem, which is illustrated in the example of two wolves and one sheep voting on what to have for dinner. In this case, as Madison put it, the rights of the sheep will be insecure. Majority rule may be democratic, but it is a bit hard on the sheep.

The core solution to these problems emerged very early in the Convention. There would be dual sovereignty. The state governments would remain with power over most government functions. In addition, a new federal government would be created and given just the power needed to manage interstate, national, and foreign issues.

In some respects, dual sovereignty is a mixture of two systems. Rather than a single national government overall, the United States has a Federal Government to handle issues involving national concerns, and then state governments, currently fifty, over everything else. The government under the constitution is a blending of a national government and a confederation of the states. This is one reason the house represents the people, while the Senate represents the states.

Dual sovereignty is also why murder is a state issue, not a federal one. Except in cases involving federal employees, there is no national murder law. This is because criminal law is something handled by the states. Not only was power divided between the states and federal governments, but the federal power would also be divided. Thus the concept of checks and balances. The idea was if one part tried to overstep its authority, the others would keep it in check.

Written towards the end of the Convention, the preamble sums up their purpose and view of government. It makes several key points and distinguishes itself from the Articles of Confederation with its opening words. The Articles were an agreement "between the states." In what became a controversy during ratification, the Constitution places the ultimate authority with "We the people," instead of "We the States." It then lists the purposes for forming,

> a more perfect union, establish Justice, insure domestic Tranquility, provide for the common defense, promote the general Welfare, and secure the Blessings of Liberty.

These reasons build off the Declaration's statement

> that all men are created equal, that they are endowed by their Creator with certain unalienable Rights, that among these are Life, Liberty and the pursuit of Happiness.--That to secure these rights, Governments are instituted among Men.

The first two reasons, "establish Justice, insure domestic Tranquility" are to protect individual rights from fellow citizens. The third, "provide for the common defense," protects from threats outside the country, while the last highlights the importance of liberty and that all rights must be secured. As for "promote the general Welfare," there would be, and continues to be, a lot of discussion on the meaning and limits of "general Welfare."

By May 29, with the preliminaries out of the way, the first order of business considered the Virginia plan. Written by Madison, it was proposed in the Convention by Edmund Randolph, then the Governor of Virginia, and thus came to be called the Virginia Plan. Randolph took most of the day introducing the plan. The next day, the committee of the whole started considering the individual parts of the Virginia plan, i.e., "a national government ought to be established consisting of a Supreme Legislative, Judiciary, and Executive."

The word 'Supreme' stood out. Its implications were clear and stark to the delegates assembled. The Convention had been called to revise the Articles, which started by saying.

> Each state retains its sovereignty, freedom, and independence, and every power, jurisdiction, and right, which is not by this Confederation expressly delegated to the United States, in Congress assembled.

The Virginia plan would fundamentally change this and could not be called a revision; it was a replacement. This broad outline passed after some debate, but many details needed to be worked out, and working out those details would take all summer. Alternatives were proposed, debated, and discarded. There would be a lot of changes. The Virginia plan's provisions would pass, then be reconsidered and rejected, only to be considered yet again and passed. These reversals were why meeting as a committee of the whole was so important. The debate was full and complete, and thanks to Madison's records, largely available today. In the end, Madison's plan became the basis for the new Constitution.

The debate was also difficult and contentious. At several points, it appeared the Convention might dissolve, unable to reach any conclusion. Some members left and never returned. The divisions were many, and at times difficult to appreciate now. At the time, loyalty to one's state was far more pronounced. Regional differences were also more pronounced.

Travel was difficult. If you lived in South Carolina, it could take longer for information to come by land from New England than by sea from England. There was also a marked difference between East and West. However, the West then had a vastly different understanding in a country consisting of states along the East Coast. Then the west included distant places like what is now the "western" part of Pennsylvania. You did not have to go far from the coast to get to the wilderness.

Probably the biggest difference was between the large and small states. The disagreements here were so strong they threatened to undermine the Convention several times. At one point, there was even a proposal made to remake the states so they would all be the same size, though few members thought that would be a workable plan.

Much of the debate followed the same general pattern. There would be two or more options. Each option would be debated, normally in terms of effectiveness versus the risk of abuse. The result would be some mixture of the options to achieve effectiveness, but with checks and balances to mitigate any abuse. For example, one proposal was to have the legislature appoint people; another was to have the President handle appointments. The Constitution has the President appoint, but the Senate approves the appointment. Power was divided to create checks and balances.

Article I – The Congress

The first of the three parts considered by the Convention, the Legislative, was also the most controversial and thus difficult. Article I takes up over half of the Constitution before the amendments, with 2294 words. The federalists saw it as the first and the most important branch as it would be the one responsible for making the laws. Madison's plan proposed two houses. The first House would elect the second House's members from candidates nominated by the state legislatures. Eventually, becoming the House of Representatives and a Senate, key details needed to be settled first. The main disagreements came down to two issues in the Virginia plan's second resolution.

> 2. Res[d] therefore that the rights of suffrage in the National Legislature ought to be proportioned to the Quotas of contribution, or to the number of free inhabitants, as the one or the other rule may seem best in different cases

This proposal was a huge change from the Articles. The Articles allowed for between two and seven delegates for each state, but gave each state only one vote. Madison's plan changed this to a proportional system where the number of votes for a state reflected the state's size, either in terms of tax revenue or the number of free persons. This change was music to the ears of delegates from the larger states but a horror for the smaller states who believed this would place them at the mercy of the large ones. They would be the sheep for the larger states wolves.

Before an agreement could be reached, a great deal of time, debate, and disagreement occurred. On Monday, June 11, Roger Sherman of Connecticut proposed a compromise, with one House based on proportional representation. The other House with one vote per state. Sherman's compromise was quickly rejected. There was a counter-proposal on Friday, June 15, the New Jersey Plan, which continued the one vote per state from the Articles. Again, more time was spent in debate and disagreement. Roger Sherman proposed another version of his compromise again in early July, resulting in even more time, debates, and disagreement. At times it looked like the Convention would dissolve, unable to reach an agreement at all. Finally, after being rejected several times, the "Great Compromise" was accepted on July 23.

The Constitution has the House based on proportional representation reflecting the people's will. It also has a Senate for the states with two Senators each, elected by the state's legislatures. This compromise protected the interests of both the people and the states. Neither side was completely happy, but that is the nature of a compromise.

It remains a contentious issue. Because of the checks and balances, the Federal government is not able to act on simple majorities. Many saw, and still see, these checks and balances as problematic and undemocratic. You see this today in calls to get rid of the filibuster, which while not in the Constitution goes back to the early days of the Senate, or in the calls to eliminate the electoral college for electing Presidents, replacing them with simple majority rule, a majority rule that the founders specifically rejected as too dangerous. Given that many issues were handled by state governments, the founders wanted something more than a majority for national issues; they wanted a broad consensus.

Just as today, the country then consisted of many different groups, each with its own interests and concerns: small states and large states, cities and farms, North and South. The federalists sought a system where one side could not dominate through a simple numerical majority. They wanted a system that forced the consideration of all concerns, which required taking all sides into account to build a consensus on what to do.

A problem with a simple majority rule is that rather than build, it often divides. If you have the numbers on your side, you no longer have to care about the other side's interests or concerns.

You have the votes, so what does it matter what the sheep think. With simple majority rule, those who disagree are people to be defeated. What matters is getting one vote more than they did.

With the system set up by the founders, you had to care. The large states could get their way in the House, the small states in the Senate, but to get anything done, both had to talk to each other and work out an acceptable compromise. Thus rather than divide and defeat, the federalist system is based on building consensus. While the federalists saw this as a good thing, it would be, and remains, a major point of contention for those who think a simple majority should be enough.

On the other hand, as the system of checks and balances has been weakened in recent years with the move to more majority rule, polarization and division have grown. Rather than seeking how to work together, the various sides seek how to defeat their opponents.

"The number of free inhabitants"

The other issue in Madison's second resolution would have more long-term ramifications. He proposed to make the legislature proportional based on "the number of free inhabitants." This resulted in the infamous Three-Fifths Compromise, which has been greatly misunderstood.

At the time of the Convention, slavery was not the clear North versus South issue it would later become. Some in the North, such as ship owners, profited from the slave trade, while some slave owners in the South felt trapped in the system and wanted abolition. It was also a time of growing awareness and changing opinions. Earlier in his life, Benjamin Franklin owned slaves, but over time came to see the evil of slavery, calling it an "atrocious debasement of human nature."[6] At the time of the Convention, Franklin was the President of a society that worked not only to

6   B. Franklin, "Address to the Public," 9 November 1789. [Online]. Available: http://www.benjamin-franklin-history.org/address-to-the-public/. [Accessed 17 9 2020]

abolish slavery but also to improve the lives of former slaves. Still, slavery remained largely a Southern issue, with a young and growing abolitionist movement in the North.

The original idea for the Three-Fifths Compromise came from a tax proposed under the Articles of Confederation government. The plan was to determine the tax obligations for the various states based on the population of men, women, and children, including slaves. The southern states objected as they considered slaves property. Including them would increase the amount of taxes southern states needed to pay.

Northern states objected that slaves in the South take the place of freemen in the North. They argued that slavery "increase the profits of a state," and thus, "the Southern colonies would have all the benefit of slaves, whilst the Northern ones would bear the burden."[7] Besides, they argued, "it is our duty to lay every discouragement on the importation of slaves." Excluding slaves would have the opposite result.[8] The North wanted all the slaves counted; the South wanted none. The compromise was in the middle. After several other ratios were rejected, eventually, they settled on three-fifths. However, the proposal still failed to achieve the unanimous support required to pass under the Articles.

The parallels were immediately apparent when the issue of proportional representation came up in the Convention. Yet now, the sides were reversed. The South wanted to count slaves, as this would give them more representatives. Northern states argued that since the slaves could not vote, they should not be counted.

Since many of the Convention's members had taken part in Congress's debates, the three-fifth compromise surfaced early. Like many other things, this was debated, accepted, and rejected many times. In the end, another compromise allowed the Convention

7   H. Taylor, "The origin and Growth of the American Consitution," 1911. [Online]. Available: https://archive.org/details/originandgrowth02tayl-goog/page/n184/mode/2up. [Accessed 17 9 2020]
8   H. Taylor, "The origin and Growth of the American Consitution," 1911. [Online]. Available: https://archive.org/details/originandgrowth02tayl-goog/page/n184/mode/2up. [Accessed 17 9 2020]

to move forward. The ratio of three-fifth would be used for both taxation and representation. Also, while it seemed a foregone conclusion that the new government would outlaw the slave trade, it was prohibited until at least 1808 to allow a transition.

Today, some argue this compromise was a stain on the Constitution and never should have been agreed to. The former is undoubtedly true; the latter is not so clear. The Constitution was never a sure thing, quite the opposite. Slavery had been an established fact that existed as the norm from the dawn of history. It has not been eradicated even today. The number of slaves in the world today, estimated by the UN to be 40 million, is larger than at the time of Constitution. At the time of the Convention, the abolitionist movement was new and growing. Many at the Convention believed, wrongly as it turned out, that slavery would die out in a few decades.

There would have been no United States without the compromise. Alternative history is always difficult. We know how hard it was for the United States to finally abolish slavery and then later abolish Jim Crow laws and establish civil rights. Given this history, it is difficult to imagine a divided America would have abolished slavery any sooner. On the other hand, it is much easier to see slavery lasting considerably longer, possibly even until today.

This is the problem with the system of consensus set up by the federalists. Often neither side get all of what they want. A half-century later, Steven Douglas, in the Lincoln Douglas debates, would argue for maintaining the compromise of free states and slave states. He claimed that the entire nation would not have been all free without the compromise, rather would have been all slave. Would that have been better? The thing about all-or-nothing approaches is that it often leaves you with nothing.

Article II – The Executive

The long debate over the Legislative branch frequently reached an impasse. Time was needed to consider and then reconsider the various proposals and to let tempers cool. When this happened, the Convention postponed the discussion on the Legislative branch and moved on to other topics. During one of these breaks on June 1, the Convention took up the Virginia Plan's proposal to create "a national executive."

Since the executive could only execute the legislative branch's laws, this branch was not considered as critical as Article I. At 1025 words, Article II is less than half the size. Still, there was room for abuse and, thus, controversies to be settled. Four issues dominated the discussion: how strong; how many; how elected; and would there be an "executive negative," the ability to block or modify laws passed by the legislative branch.

Again, competing concerns dominated. For the executive, the competing concerns were effectiveness vs. monarchy, an executive strong enough to do what is needed but not strong enough to become a monarch. On the question of how many, one, two, or three presidents were considered. Having more than one President would certainly make establishing a monarchy more difficult. It also solves the problem of having a President who dies in office; on the other hand, having more than one would lead to problems when disagreements arise. There was also the issue of accountability; who is responsible if there is more than one? The Constitution has a single President elected to a four-year term and who could be impeached by the Legislative branch. There would also be a Vice President who could take over if the President died in office.

Again, many different options were considered, debated, accepted, only to be rejected when reconsidered for electing the President. Should a direct vote of the people elect the President? Should Congress select the President? Should electors chosen by state legislatures choose the President? The same small versus large states debate emerged. The most populous states would pick the President if done by popular vote. The smaller states would effectively have no say and could easily be ignored. How can the

29

President be a national official if only a few large states are needed for election?

Letting Congress pick the President also had a problem. That meant the executive branch would be accountable to the legislative, weakening the divided powers' checks and balances. Finally, after much debate and 60 different votes, the Constitution has the President elected by the electoral college, whose electors are chosen by the people. Over time this morphed into the system that we have today that mixes simple majority rule within states with the electoral college to achieve consensus. All states have a say, not just the large population centers.

Alexander Hamilton

The ability of the President to veto legislation was also a point of disagreement. On the one hand, it was seen as an important check on the legislative branch. On the other, a potential source for abuse and even corruption. Franklin spoke of his experience with the Governor's veto in Pennsylvania, where "No good law whatever could be passed without private bargain with him."[9] In

9   C. D. Bowen, *Miracle at Philadelphia*, New York: Little, Brown and Company, 1966, p 60

the final compromise, the President has the veto but allows the veto to be overridden by Congress.

Article III –The Judiciary

Article III specifies there would be a single Supreme Court and other "inferior Courts as the Congress may from time to time ordain and establish." Of the three branches of government, the Convention spent the least amount of time on the judiciary. At a mere 377 words in length, it is about a third of Article II and a sixth the size of Article I. It was important, but, as Hamilton wrote in Federalist 78,

> It proves incontestably, that the judiciary is beyond comparison the weakest of the three departments of power; that it can never attack with success either of the other two; and that all possible care is requisite to enable it to defend itself against their attacks.

The courts were seen as a check primarily on the other two branches and a defense for the Constitution. Hamilton went on to write,

> The complete independence of the courts of justice is peculiarly essential in a limited Constitution. By a limited Constitution, I understand one which contains certain specified exceptions to the legislative authority; such, for instance, as that it shall pass no bills of attainder, no ex post facto laws, and the like. Limitations of this kind can be preserved in practice no other way than through the medium of courts of justice, whose duty it must be to declare all acts contrary to the manifest tenor of the Constitution void.

It is sometimes argued the ability to declare laws unconstitutional was created in *Marbury v. Madison* (1803). Yet, Hamilton argued for that role in Federalist 78.

While the courts were not considered a threat, Hamilton pointed out, "that as liberty can have nothing to fear from the judiciary alone, but would have everything to fear from its union with either of the other departments." It is for this reason the Courts are not dependent on the other branches. Hamilton argues,

> If, then, the courts of justice are to be considered as the bulwarks of a limited Constitution against legislative encroachments, this consideration will afford a strong argument for the permanent tenure of judicial offices, since nothing will contribute so much as this to that independent spirit in the judges which must be essential to the faithful performance of so arduous a duty.

As for the danger of the Court using its position to make law, has Hamilton wrote in Federalist 81,

> It may in the last place be observed that the supposed danger of judiciary encroachments on the legislative authority, which has been upon many occasions reiterated, is in reality a phantom. Particular misconstructions and contraventions of the will of the legislature may now and then happen; but they can never be so extensive as to amount to an inconvenience, or in any sensible degree to affect the order of the political system.

This latter prediction by Hamilton would be called into question in the coming century.

Article IV-VII

The four remaining Articles (657 words) address various other issues. Article IV deals with the relationships between the states and says citizens from different states must be treated equally. In practice, this means those married in one state would be considered married in others, or in more modern terms, a Driver's License issued in one state is valid in all states.

It also handles admitting new states. Even here there was controversy. The Northwest Ordinance, often called the third most important document in the founding of the country, was enacted by the Congress of the Confederation in the middle of the Convention. The Northwest Territory mainly composed the land that now make up the states of Ohio, Indiana, Illinois, Michigan and Wisconsin. Article 5 of the ordinance stated, "There shall be formed in the said territory, not less than three nor more than five States." It went on to state that, whenever any of the said States shall have sixty thousand free inhabitants therein, such State shall be admitted, by its delegates, into the Congress of the United States, on an equal footing with the original States in all respects whatever, and shall be at liberty to form a permanent constitution and State government: Provided, the constitution and government so to be formed, shall be republican, and in conformity to the principles contained in these articles.

This was all well and good, but now the articles were going away. In addition, some at the Convention did not like the Northwest Ordinance. They objected to new, particularly western, states entering the union on an equal basis.

In the end, after again a lot of discussion, the general principles of the Northwest Ordinance were adopted by the convention including the mandate that all states have a republican form of government, that is, a government accountable to its citizens.

Article V provides for amendments to the Constitution. You can see the distrust between the large and small states in that it also guarantees each State an equal vote in the Senate.

Article VI deals with previous debts and establishes the Constitution and Federal Law as the "supreme Law of the Land." This latter clause would be a frequent issue in American history, up to and including the present day. It arises whenever various local and state governments disagree with Federal Law and try to go their own way. Article VI also requires officials to take an oath or make an affirmation, "to support this Constitution; but no religious Test shall ever be required as a Qualifications to any Office or public Trust under the United States."

Finally, with Article VII, the Constitution specified only nine States would be needed for ratification.

In summary, the Convention's story is a story of debate, long, often heated, and at times, even abusive. Several times the disagreement was so great it looked as if the Convention might dissolve in failure. At one of these dark moments on June 28, Franklin rose to move "that henceforth prayers imploring the assistance of heaven and its blessings on our deliberation." Roger Sherman immediately seconded the motion. Other delegates were concerned that suddenly bringing in a clergyman this far into the Convention might be seen as a sign of problems, which frankly it was. However, there was a bigger problem. Madison's notes records, "Mr. WILLIAMSON, observed that the true cause of the omission could not be mistaken. The Convention had no funds."

In the end, the story of the Constitution is also a story of compromise. Only a few of the issues have been highlighted here. There were many more that were fought over. Virtually every provision resulted in a disagreement needing to be resolved. It is a story of many interests coming together and seeking to balance many different and often conflicting concerns. The only reason it had any chance at all was that most members agreed the Articles were unworkable and no union would be worse. Everything was debated, considered, the pros and cons discussed, passed, then rejected until a compromise could be crafted. Nobody got everything they wanted. Everyone gave up something.

These compromises are the reasons the Constitution was so successful. As a result of all these compromises, checks, and balances, the resulting Constitution creates a truly national government where no single group could dominate. Sovereignty was divided between the federal government and the states. The federal government was limited to certain enumerated powers, basically concerning interstate, national and foreign issues.

The government that people would encounter the most would be their state or even local government. Individual states were free to pass laws for their states. Large urban states could pass the laws they felt they needed, while the small rural states could pass the ones they needed.

That they were different from state to state was expected. Life in rural Montana is different than in New York City. A law that makes sense in one area may not fit another. National laws, however, would require a national consensus. Accomplishing anything at the national level requires agreement from a wide range of groups, essentially from the nation as a whole, not just the large population centers.

This general debate continues even today. Some see this forcing of a national consensus as a problem, but it was a key factor in the Constitution. The large groups believe they should control everything if they have fifty percent plus one. The smaller rural areas don't understand why they should be governed by people who live in far-off cities with little understanding of their lives. So the debate continues.

Given all the difficulties and differences, the delegates reaching any agreement seemed unlikely. Less so that it would last as long as it has. As such, the Convention, and the Constitution they produced, have been called The Miracle at Philadelphia.

The Bill of Rights

The Convention was nearing its end. The major issues had been settled; everyone was exhausted. The heat of the summer and the long debates had taken their toll. The Convention would only meet four more days when George Mason rose and said he "wished the plan had been prefaced with a Bill of Rights."[10] It was too late to be introducing what everyone knew would be no simple matter, and the motion to form a committee was nearly unanimously defeated.

It was not just the lateness of the date that defeated the motion. Many delegates believed the new Constitution limited the government's role such that no statement of rights was needed. They also believed a statement of rights would be counterproductive as it could never be complete. Any right not mentioned would not be recognized. In short, they saw a bill of rights as limiting rights just to those mentioned.

Mason was correct; the new Constitution would need a Bill of Rights. Before long, Madison, who had opposed a Bill of

10   J. Madison, "IN CONVENTION," 12 9 1787. [Online]. Available: https://www.nhccs.org/dfc-0912.txt. [Accessed 17 9 2020]

Rights, came to realize without it, the new Constitution would never be ratified. He changed to become an advocate. It was too late to add it to the Constitution, so he argued it should be one of the first issues taken up by the new Congress, and it was. The Bill of Rights passed out of Congress along with two other changes, twelve amendments in all. Only amendments three through 12 comprising the Bill of Rights would be initially approved by the states. We will discuss the fate of the other two later.

The New Government

With New Hampshire voting to ratify the new Constitution on June 21, 1788, the nine states needed had ratified the Constitution. The new government came into existence on March 4, 1789. There was never any question of who the first President would be, and George Washington was sworn in on April 30, 1789. Washington set the pattern for the presidency. As a new office, he established many of the norms and conventions that defined the role for years to come, including voluntarily stepping down after two terms, though he could have easily served for life.

The first real contested presidential election occurred between John Adams and Thomas Jefferson. Adams, then the Vice President, won, and since Washington was stepping aside, there was no issue with the transfer of power. The election of 1800 posed a different concern. Adams and Jefferson ran again; Adams, as part of the new Federalist Party, and Jefferson, now called a Democratic-Republican,[11] were bitter opponents. Unlike the previous election, this time Jefferson won. However, in one of the more difficult elections in U.S. history, he tied with Aaron Burr. The election was thrown into the House, which eventually picked Jefferson.

---

11   Technically they were called the Republican Party, but this cause confusion with the modern Republican party. Just as the federalist would become the Whigs, and then the modern Republican Party, this Republican Party would in time become the Democrat party. Therefore, to avoid confusion it is called the Democrat-Republican Party.

While British parliaments had been changing hands for well over a century, this was something new, the peaceful transfer of power for a head of state. The head of state would be replaced by a bitter political opponent yet agreeing to give up power. That this transfer followed a messy election is even more astounding. But Adams stepped down, and Jefferson became President. The Constitutional system was tested, and it worked.

The 19th Century: Structure Becomes Practice (1801-1901)

With the new century, the Constitution was in place and had survived its first test. Still, there were a lot of details to be worked out and understood. For the most part, this fell to the Courts, and the controversies began right from the start. Could a citizen of one state sue the government of another state? This question came to the Supreme Court in *Chisholm v. Georgia* (1793), in which the majority ruled they could. While the ruling was correct, it was still seen as a problem and was quickly fixed with the 11th amendment ratified in 1795.

The next major case is also one of the most important cases for the Court, *Marbury v. Madison* in 1803. It also highlights an important distinction often overlooked in the coverage of the Court today. There is a difference between the ruling and the reasoning; between what they ruled and why they ruled. For the participants in a lawsuit, the 'what' is clearly the most important. Did they win or lose? But for the Constitution and the country, the why is far more important. Nowhere is this clearer than in *Marbury v. Madison*. Many know the reasoning and why it is important, but far fewer know what was at issue in the case or how the court ruled on that issue.

The case came out of the messy 1800 election. While power was peacefully transferred, that did not mean it was happily transferred. The outgoing Federalist party tried to hamper the incoming Democrat-Republicans. One outcome of this was William Marbury and others nominated and confirmed as justices of the peace in the District of Columbia never received their actual commissions. They sued in the Supreme Court, asking the Court to order Secretary of State James Madison to deliver the commissions. This type of order is called a *writ of mandamus*, and Congress had specifically given the Court this power in the Judiciary Act of 1789.

The Court ruled the commission's delivery was a mere formality, and its absence did not invalidate the appointment. The Court also ruled Marbury was entitled to a legal remedy. These would indicate a ruling in favor of Marbury. Instead, the Court said they could not issue the writ, and their reasoning is what makes this case so important. In considering whether the Court could grant the writ, Chief Justice Marshall wrote,

> The powers of the legislature are defined and limited; and that those limits may not be mistaken or forgotten, the constitution is written. To what purpose are powers limited, and to what purpose is that limitation committed to writing; if these limits may, at any time, be passed by those intended to be restrained? The distinction between a government with limited and unlimited powers is abolished, if those limits do not confine the persons on whom they are imposed, and if acts prohibited and acts allowed are of equal obligation. It is a proposition too plain to be contested, that the constitution controls any legislative act repugnant to it; or, that the legislature may alter the constitution by an ordinary act.
>
> Between these alternatives there is no middle ground. The constitution is either a superior, paramount law, unchangeable by ordinary means, or it is on a level with ordinary legislative acts, and like other acts, is alterable when the legislature shall please to alter.

While the Judiciary Act of 1789 gave the Court the power to issue the writ, the Court held the Act invalid. Congress could not give the Supreme Court powers not given it by the Constitution. As Marshall wrote, "the law is unconstitutional, and therefore absolutely incapable of conferring the authority, and assigning the duties which its words purport to confer and assign." Marshall went on to write,

> It is emphatically the province and duty of the judicial department to say what the law is. Those who apply the rule to particular cases, must of necessity expound and interpret that rule. If two laws conflict with each other, the courts must decide on the operation of each.

In his ruling, some falsely believe that Marshall created the concept of Judicial Review, i.e., the ability to rule a law unconstitutional. As we saw earlier, Hamilton argued for that role in Federalist 78. While Marshall's opinion did not create the concept of Judicial Review, it did make it explicit and also a "duty of the judicial department."

A Slave Auction

Another fallout from the 1800 election was the realization that having the Vice President be the second-place finisher in the presidential election was not a good idea. The 12th amendment, ratified in 1804, changed this, so both the President and Vice President are elected. With the ratification of the 12th amendment, many of the Constitution's initial flaws had been fixed. Still, one issue remained, and it would continue to surface, straining the government to the point of breaking.

Slavery.

Any hopes slavery would disappear were dashed as attitudes in the South changed. Many of the founding fathers, even some in the South, saw slavery as a moral problem. They struggled with the best way to eliminate it. In the seventh and last of the Lincoln Douglas debates, as Lincoln moved to close, he argued that slavery

will be placed again where the wisest and best men of the world placed it. Brooks of South Carolina once declared that when this Constitution was framed, its framers did not look to the institution existing until this day. When he said this, I think he stated a fact that is fully borne out by the history of the times. But he also said they were better and wiser men than the men of these days; yet the men of these days had experience which they had not, and by the invention of the cotton-gin it became a necessity in this country that slavery should be perpetual. I now say that, willingly or unwillingly, purposely or without purpose, Judge Douglas has been the most prominent instrument in changing the position of the institution of slavery which the fathers of the Government expected to come to an end ere this,—and putting it upon Brooks's cotton-gin basis; placing it where he openly confesses he has no desire there shall ever be an end of it.

Abraham Lincoln

The new view that arose in the early part of the 19th century did not simply resist abolition but sought to justify slavery as a good thing. In doing so, they began to question the very premise upon which the country had been founded. Perhaps the foremost defender of this view was John C. Calhoun.

Born in South Carolina, Calhoun was active in politics from his election to the House of Representatives in 1810. He served as Secretary of War, Secretary of State, was Vice President for both John Quincy Adams and then Adams' political opponent and successor Andrew Jackson. He ended his career as a Senator from South Carolina until he died in 1850.

For Calhoun, slavery was not a necessary evil but a positive good. He rejected the Declaration of Independence, for he recognized the transformational quality of its claim,

> that all men are created equal, that they are endowed by their Creator with certain unalienable Rights, that among these are Life, Liberty and the pursuit of Happiness.

John C. Calhoun

The problem was he did not like the transformation he was seeing. During the summer of 1848, the Senate debated a bill establishing a government for the Oregon territory. This territory was much larger than the current state, covering the northwest coast eastward into parts of present-day Montana and Wyoming. Whether a new territory or a new state, the issue of slavery always came up. Would this area be slave or free?

In his speech on the bill, Calhoun argued against the "erroneous" claim all men are created equal found in the Declaration.

He argued the error had germinated and was now producing fruit, i.e., limits on slavery.

> We now begin to experience the danger of admitting so great an error to have a place in the Declaration of our independence. For a long time it lay dormant; but in the process of time it began to germinate, and produce its poisonous fruits. It had strong hold on the mind of Mr. Jefferson, the author of that document, which caused him to take an utterly false view of the subordinate relation of the black to the white race in the South; and to hold, in consequence, that the latter, though utterly unqualified to possess liberty, were as fully entitled to both liberty and equality as the former; and that to deprive them of it was unjust and immoral.

From a historical perspective, it is important to note Calhoun's rejection of the Declaration of Independence because of its claim that all men are created equal. He called it a great error. Later some like Steven Douglas in the Lincoln Douglas Debates would attempt to reconcile the Declaration's claim with the existence of slavery by claiming the men in this statement only included white men. Yet, it seems clear that Calhoun never heard of or even considered this option. If he had, he certainly would have adopted it. Calhoun believed the Declaration's claim did include all men, which being a racist, is why he considered it "so great an error to have a place in the Declaration of our independence."

In addition, for Calhoun, liberty was not a right that the government was to protect but a reward that government could bestow on some, but not on others.

> Instead, then, of liberty and equality being born with men,—instead of all men and all classes and descriptions being equally entitled to them, they are high prizes to be won, and are in their most perfect state, not only the highest reward that can be bestowed on our race, but the most difficult to be won,—and when won, the most difficult to be preserved.

The conflict between the Declaration's view and the new view that saw slavery as something good was fought through the first half of the century, resulting in states being admitted in pairs, one slave and one free. There was the Missouri Compromise (1820-21) and the Kansas-Nebraska Act (1854), the latter resulting in a series of violent confrontations referred to as Bleeding Kansas. Still, the inherent conflict between the principle upon which the country was founded, and the existence of slavery, prohibited a final resolution.

This conflict led Abraham Lincoln, who had just been nominated the Republican candidate for Senate, to give his now famous House Divided speech in which he predicted,

> We are now far into the fifth year, since a policy was initiated, with the avowed object, and confident promise, of putting an end to slavery agitation. Under the operation of that policy, that agitation has not only, not ceased, but has constantly augmented. In my opinion, it will not cease, until a crisis shall have been reached, and passed. "A house divided against itself cannot stand." I believe this government cannot endure, permanently half slave and half free. I do not expect the Union to be dissolved -- I do not expect the House to fall -- but I do expect it will cease to be divided. It will become all one thing or all the other. Either the opponents of slavery, will arrest the further spread of it, and place it where the public mind shall rest in the belief that it is in the course of ultimate extinction; or its advocates will push it forward, till it shall become alike lawful in all the States, old as well as new -- North as well as South.

Dred Scott

44

In his speech, Lincoln also mentioned the Dred Scott decision of the previous year as one of the things bringing the issue of slavery to a head. Dred Scott was a slave owned by a U.S. Army surgeon Dr. John Emerson. Dr. Emerson took Scott with him when serving in free territories. Scott eventually filed suit, claiming that while in the territory where slavery was prohibited, he had become a free man. After working its way through the courts, and with a change in ownership and a misspelling of the new owner's name, the case eventually reached the Supreme court as *Dred Scott v. Sandford.*

The Court ruled 7-2 against Scott. In the first part of the majority opinion written by Chief Justice Roger Taney, the Court ruled that Scott, as "one of the African race," could not be a citizen. This was not a statement grounded in the Declaration of Independence or the Constitution. This claim was something new. Taney used his racism rather than these documents to reach this decision. In his dissent, Justice Curtis rejected the claim the Constitution was a document for the white race, pointing out as a factual matter,

> It has already been shown that in five of the thirteen original States, colored persons then possessed the elective franchise, and were among those by whom the Constitution was ordained and established. If so, it is not true, in point of fact, that the Constitution was made exclusively by the white race. And that it was made exclusively for the white race is, in my opinion, not only an assumption not warranted by anything in the Constitution, but contradicted by its opening declaration, that it was ordained and established by the people of the United States, for themselves and their posterity.

This part of the ruling should have ended the case. This case was only in the Supreme Court because Scott and Sanford (Sandford) were citizens of different states. Yet, if Scott was not a citizen as Taney ruled, the Court had no basis upon which to proceed. Yet, Taney took on the Legislative role that Hamilton in Federalist

81 had thought was "in reality a phantom." So, proceed, Taney did.

Taney ruled that Scott, as a slave, was mere property, and Congress had no power to restrict slavery. By doing so, Taney effectively invalidated the earlier compromises and created a constitutional right to slavery. As Constitutional scholar Robert Bork summarized this opinion,

> How did Taney know that slave ownership was a constitutional right? Such a right is nowhere to be found in the Constitution. He knew it because he was passionately convinced that it *must* be a constitutional right."[12] (original emphasis)

The division between free and slave states would have disappeared if allowed to stand and followed to its logical conclusion. In fact, just what the court would do next came up as part of the Lincoln Douglas Debate.   Taney tried to settle the slavery issue that had plagued the country since its founding and used his power on the Supreme Court to do so. Instead of settling the issue, he only exacerbated matters leading to the Civil War two years later.

Reconstruction

Tensions remained with the end of the war. There was the desire among more moderate Republicans and Northern Democrats to heal the nation and readmit the southern states. More radical Republicans pushed to ensure full civil rights for the former slaves. With a lot of help from Lincoln, the 13th amendment (1865) passed and abolished slavery. Still, the principles of the Declaration remained an unachieved goal, and while slavery was banned, the issue of race remained. Southern states began passing Black Code laws, limiting the newly granted freedoms. These laws had the unintended consequence of strengthening the Radical Republicans' arguments and resulted in the passage of the 14th amendment (1868).

---

12   R. H. Bork, *The Tempting of America*, New York: The Free Press, 1990, p 31

The 14th amendment effectively overruled the Supreme Court's Dred Scott ruling that Africans could not be citizens. It also tried to enshrine many of the rights recently passed by Congress into the Constitution, in theory shielding them from future Congresses. It tried to do this by taking the rights granted under the Constitution and extending them to the state governments, with the Privileges and Immunities Clause, the Due Process clause, and the Equal Protection clause. Even then, not trusting the states, they added an enforcement clause. The exact meaning of these clauses would be fought out in the courts in years to come.

After he became President, Ulysses S. Grant supported passing several civil rights bills to give Blacks more freedom and to permit the federal government to go after groups like the Ku Klux Klan. They were successful, largely driving the Klan out of existence, though they would stage a comeback in 50 years. Grant also supported the adoption of the 15th amendment (1870), which prohibited restricting voting "on account of race, color, or previous condition of servitude." It would be 43 years before there would be another amendment.

It did not take long for the meaning of the new amendments to be questioned in the courts. A series of cases, the Slaughter-House Cases (1873), *Bradwell v. Illinois* (1873), and *United States v. Cruikshank* (1875), virtually eliminated the Privileges and Immunities Clause. In the Civil Rights Cases (1883), the Court limited applying the 14th amendment to a state's actions, excluding private individuals' actions.

The election of 1876 was one of the most controversial in American history. It was finally settled in Congress with the Compromise of 1877. Hayes would become the President, and Reconstruction and federal efforts to enforce civil rights would end in exchange. Southern states quickly expanded their efforts to restrict the freedom of Blacks through Jim Crow laws, named after a character in a Black minstrel show.

In 1880 Louisiana passed a law requiring separate but equal rail cars for Blacks and whites. While separate in practice, normally, they were equal only in theory. Homer Plessy was arrested for sitting in the wrong car and found guilty by Judge John Ferguson. In *Plessy v. Ferguson* (1896), the Supreme Court upheld Plessy's conviction enshrining separate but equal into the Constitution for the next 60 years. In the lone dissent Justice John Marshall Harlan, who also dissented from the Civil Rights Cases (1883), wrote,

> But in view of the constitution, in the eye of the law, there is in this country no superior, dominant, ruling class of citizens. There is no caste here. Our constitution is color-blind, and neither knows nor tolerates classes among citizens. In respect of civil rights, all citizens are equal before the law. The humblest is the peer of the most powerful. The law regards man as man, and takes no account of his surroundings or of his color when his civil rights as guaranteed by the supreme law of the land are involved.

Justice Harlan went on to predict, "in my opinion, the judgment this day rendered will, in time, prove to be quite as pernicious as the decision made by this tribunal in the Dred Scott Case." He was proved correct. While the other cases are still considered "good law," both *Dred Scott* and *Plessy v. Ferguson* are considered anti-canon by virtually all modern legal scholars, mistakes by the Court.

In the latter half of the 19th century, a new movement took shape, again questioning the Declaration's validity and the federalists' understanding of the Constitution. The movement, progressivism, would come to shape much of our understanding of government in the next century through the present day.

The Progressive Era: Rejection, Transformation, and Change (1901-1964)

The election of 1900 did not appear to be momentous in any way. William McKinley was seeking his second term in a rematch with Williams Jennings Bryan. Economic times were good, and the recent victory in the Spanish-American War, along with a war hero for a running mate, gave McKinley a comfortable margin of victory. Six months into his second term, McKinley was shot by an anarchist while shaking hands in Buffalo, New York. He died eight days later.

Theodore Roosevelt became President and, in doing so, brought progressivism to the White House. With it, he brought a new way of looking at the Constitution, ultimately changing how our government works. For progressives, the Constitution, with its structure of checks and balances, was outdated. Roosevelt believed in "certain new 'checks and balances which may check and balance the special interests and their allies."[13]

The Founding Fathers had been a product of the enlightenment; the progressives were likewise a product of their time. Whereas the Founding Father's views grew out of the enlighten-

---

13 T. Roosevelt, "The Right of the People to Rule," 20 3 1912. [Online]. Available: https://teachingamericanhistory.org/library/document/the-rights-of-the-people-to-rule-2/. [Accessed 6 10 2020]

ment ideas of Locke and Montesquieu, Progressives' intellectual history traced back more to the French Revolution and Jean-Jacques Rousseau, a later enlightenment thinker who at times challenged more traditional enlightenment philosophical views.

Rousseau rejected the enlightenment views of reason and the individual. Rousseau agreed with other enlightenment thinkers that reason was the basis for civilization. The problem was he did not like civilization,

> Metallurgy and agriculture were the two arts whose invention produced this great revolution. With the poet, it is gold and silver, but with the philosopher it is iron and corn, which have civilized men, and ruined mankind.[14]

Rather than focusing on individuals and rights like the federalists, Rousseau was more concerned with groups and equality.

As a result, progressives questioned many of the principles upon which the Constitution was based. They also took a different view of how government should be structured and operate. These differences can be summarized as differences over human nature, government's purpose, the need for checks and balances, direct democracy, who should rule, and rights.

Theodore Roosevelt

Human Nature

The federalists accepted the general view that human nature was fixed and flawed. It was a mixture of good and bad, and the bad was something to be guarded against. Again, this was perhaps best summed by Madison in Federalist 51,

---

14   J.-J. Rousseau, *Discourse on The Origin of Inequality*, 1755

It may be a reflection on human nature, that such devices should be necessary to control the abuses of government. But what is government itself but the greatest of all reflections on human nature? If men were angels, no government would be necessary. If angels were to govern men, neither external nor internal controls on government would be necessary. In framing a government which is to be administered by men over men, the great difficulty lies in this: You must first enable the government to control the governed; and in the next place, oblige it to control itself. A dependence on the people is no doubt the primary control on the government; but experience has taught mankind the necessity of auxiliary precautions.

Progressives rejected this view. Following in the footsteps of Rousseau, the problems the federalists attributed to human nature; the progressives saw more as problems with society. If you could perfect society, you would perfect humanity.

The early progressive intellectual Herbert Croly argued in his book, *The Promise of American Life*, that government not only could perfect human nature, it must do so to be successful.

Jean-Jacques Rousseau

Democracy must stand or fall on a platform of possible human perfectibility. If human nature cannot be improved by institutions, democracy is at best a more than usually safe form of political organization; and the only interesting inquiry about its future would be: How long will it continue to work? But if it is to work better as well as merely longer, it must have some leavening effect on human nature; and the sincere democrat is obliged to assume the power of the leaven.

51

In short, human nature can be perfected. It is the job of government leaders to construct a society that will make this happen.

Government's Purpose

The federalists embraced enlightenment values as expressed in the Declaration. People had rights grounded in Natural Law, and these rights are fixed and cannot be changed. Times and circumstances would change, but the rights of the people would not; they could only be protected or violated. The purpose of government is to protect those rights from internal and external threats, yet do so without becoming a threat to the very rights it was trying to protect.

Progressives rejected this view, seeking instead a government whose purpose would evolve as society changed, a government that sought progress with the times. Protecting rights may have been the right goal in the eighteenth and early nineteenth centuries. Still, the government should have other goals in the early twentieth. Frank Goodnow, an early progressive intellectual, wrote,

> The political philosophy of the eighteenth century was formulated before the announcement and acceptance of the theory of evolutionary development. The natural rights doctrine presupposed almost that society was static or stationary rather than dynamic or progressive in character.[15]

Goodnow expressed his view as,

> We no longer believe as we once believed that a good social organization can be secured merely through stressing our rights... But we have come to the conclusion that man under modern conditions is primarily a member of society and that only as he recognizes his duties as a member of society can he secure the greatest opportunities as an individual. While we do not regard society as an end in itself we do consider it as one

15   F. Goodnow, "The American Conception of Liberty," 1916. [Online]. Available: http://www.nlnrac.org/critics/american-progressivism/primary-source-documents/american-conception-of-liberty. [Accessed 6 10 2020]

of the most important means through which man may come into his own.[16]

Woodrow Wilson, running for President in 1912, continued this line of argument,

> The laws of this country have not kept up with the change of economic circumstances in this country; they have not kept up with the change of political circumstances; and therefore we are not even where we were when we started... I am, therefore, forced to be a progressive, if for no other reason, because we have not kept up with our changes of conditions, either in the economic field or in the political field.[17]

Wilson went on to talk about how the Federalists' view was built on a Newtonian view of the world, but Darwin would govern the modern.

Woodrow Wilson

> And they constructed a government as they would have constructed an orrery,–to display the laws of nature. Politics in their thought was a variety of mechanics. The Constitution was founded on the law of gravitation. The government was to exist and move by virtue of the efficacy of "checks and balances." The trouble with the theory is that government is not a machine, but a living thing. It falls, not under the theory of the universe, but under the theory of organic life. It is accountable to Darwin, not to Newton.[18]

16   F. Goodnow, "The American Conception of Liberty," 1916. [Online]. Available: http://www.nlnrac.org/critics/american-progressivism/primary-source-documents/american-conception-of-liberty. [Accessed 6 10 2020]
17   W. Wilson, "What is Progress," 1912. [Online]. Available: https://constitutingamerica.org/what-is-progress-by-woodrow-wilson-1856-1924-reprinted-from-the-u-s-constitution-a-reader-published-by-hillsdale-college/. [Accessed 6 10 2020]
18   W. Wilson, "What is Progress," 1912. [Online]. Available: https://constitutingamerica.org/what-is-progress-by-woodrow-wilson-1856-1924-reprinted-from-the-u-s-constitution-a-reader-published-by-hillsdale-college/. [Accessed 6 10 2020].

Of course, the progressive view ran counter to Lincoln's view concerning the centrality of the Declaration of Independence. They saw it as only having historical significance. This conflict did not go unnoticed by progressives such as Wilson. He went on to argue that,

> Some citizens of this country have never got beyond the Declaration of Independence, signed in Philadelphia, July 4, 1776. Their bosoms swell against George III, but they have no consciousness of the War for freedom that is going on today. The Declaration of Independence did not mention the questions of our day. It is of no consequence to us unless we can translate its general terms into examples of the present day.[19]

This was a much more expansive view of government. In this view, the government's concerns go far beyond protecting individuals' natural rights and include economic results. Accordingly, Croly argued,

> A democracy has as much interest in regulating for its own benefit the distribution of economic power as it has the distribution of political power, and the consequences of ignoring this interest would be as fatal in one case as in the other.[20]

The Need for Checks and Balances

These different views of human nature and the government's role and purpose had ramifications, particularly regarding the need for a limited government with checks and balances. Wilson objected to the notion of checks and balances because the government was more like a living thing than a machine,

> No living thing can have its organs offset against each other, as checks, and live. On the contrary, its life is dependent upon their quick cooperation, their ready

19   W. Wilson, "What is Progress," 1912. [Online]. Available: https://constitutingamerica.org/what-is-progress-by-woodrow-wilson-1856-1924-reprinted-from-the-u-s-constitution-a-reader-published-by-hillsdale-college/. [Accessed 6 10 2020].
20   H. Croly, "The Promise of American Life," 11 1909. [Online]. Available: https://www.gutenberg.org/files/14422/14422-h/14422-h.htm. [Accessed 8 10 2020].

> response to the commands of instinct or intelligence, their amicable community of purpose. Government is not a body of blind forces; it is a body of men... Their cooperation is indispensable, their warfare fatal. There can be no successful government without the intimate, instinctive coordination of the organs of life and action.

Rather than a protection against the danger of tyranny, checks and balances were themselves seen as dangerous. They kept the government restricted and unable to act as needed to keep up with society's changes.

Direct Democracy

Closely related to the different views of checks and balances is the difference over direct or pure democracy, about which the federalists were very concerned. As Alexander Hamilton summed up in a speech at the New York Ratifying Convention,

> It has been observed by an honorable gentleman, that a pure democracy, if it were practicable, would be the most perfect government. Experience has proved, that no position in politics is more false than this. The ancient democracies, in which the people themselves deliberated, never possessed one feature of good government. Their very character was tyranny.[21]

Again, the progressives disagreed. Herbert Croly argued,

> After centuries of political development, in which certain forms of representation were imposed upon progressive nations by conditions of practical efficiency, and in which these representative forms grew continually in variety and complexity, underlying conditions have again shifted. Pure democracy has again become not merely possible, but natural and appropriate.[22]

Theodore Roosevelt echoed this view while on the campaign trail in 1912 saying,

---

21 A. Hamilton, "New York Ratifying Convention. First Speech of June 21 (Francis Childs's Version), [21 June 1788]," 21 6 1787. [Online]. Available: https://founders.archives.gov/documents/Hamilton/01-05-02-0012-0011. [Accessed 6 10 2020]
22 Edited by the Hillsdale College Politics Faculty, *The U.S. Constitution: A Reader*, Hillsdale, Michigan: Hillsdale College Press. Kindle Edition., 2012, p. 694

> I have scant patience with this talk of the tyranny of the majority. Wherever there is tyranny of the majority, I shall protest against it with all my heart and soul. But we are today suffering from the tyranny of minorities.[23]

So in the question of majority rule versus building a national consensus, the progressives came down on the side of majority rule. However, they did not completely dismiss the problems that concerned the Federalists. Instead, they had a different answer.

Who Should Rule

The federalists very carefully set up a system of dual sovereignty and divided power with checks and balances, where ultimate authority always rested with the people. The government could grow and change, but if the people did not like what was happening, they could vote for a change. If one part of government got out of control, people could vote for other parts to block them. A major reason for a single executive was there would be one person the people could hold accountable.

Despite the push for direct or pure democracy, progressives did not fully trust the majority and so believed much of government, what they called administration, needed to be removed from politics and thus from the people's control. As Wilson wrote,

> Most important to be observed is the truth already so much and so fortunately insisted upon by our civil-service reformers; namely, that administration lies outside the proper sphere of politics. Administrative questions are not political questions. Although politics sets the tasks for administration, it should not be suffered to manipulate its offices.[24]

As their name implies, progressives sought progress through the reform of government. But here, the very same people they sought to serve could be a barrier. Wilson argued,

23   T. Roosevelt, "The Right of the People to Rule," 20 3 1912. [Online]. Available: https://teachingamericanhistory.org/library/document/the-rights-of-the-people-to-rule-2/. [Accessed 6 10 2020]
24   W. Wilson, "The Study of Administration," 6 1887. [Online]. Available: https://archive.org/details/jstor-2139277/page/n1/mode/2up. [Accessed 7 10 2020]

> In government, as in virtue, the hardest of hard things is to make progress. Formerly the reason for this was that the single person who was sovereign was generally either selfish, ignorant, timid, or a fool,—albeit there was now and again one who was wise. Nowadays the reason is that the many, the people, who are sovereign have no single ear which one can approach, and are selfish, ignorant, timid, stubborn, or foolish with the selfishness, the ignorances, the stubbornnesses, the timidities, or the follies of several thousand persons,—albeit there are hundreds who are wise.[25]

As such, much of Congress's actual legislative role was to move to executive agencies under the control of administrators, insulated from the politics and thus the people.

Rights

The federalists' view of rights was grounded in the concept that "all men are created equal." The rights specified in the Bill of Rights reflected rights "endowed by their Creator" that the government was to protect. For progressives, these rights were not sufficient and, in some cases, were not even the most important. As Croly wrote, "The best that can be said on behalf of this traditional American system of political ideas is that it contained the germ of better things." This system "did not constitute a progressive and formative political principle."[26] Because of their intellectual roots, Progressives were more concerned with equality, and here individual rights could be a problem. Croly argues that the federalist view of rights

> seem wholly blind to the fact that under a legal system which holds private property sacred there may be equal rights, but there cannot possibly be any equal opportunities for exercising such rights. The chance which the individual has to compete with his fellows and take a prize in the race is vitally affected by material conditions over which he has no control.

25   W. Wilson, "The Study of Administration," 6 1887. [Online]. Available: https://archive.org/details/jstor-2139277/page/n1/mode/2up. [Accessed 7 10 2020]
26   H. Croly, "The Promise of American Life," 11 1909. [Online]. Available: https://www.gutenberg.org/files/14422/14422-h/14422-h.htm. [Accessed 8 10 2020]

Progressives were troubled by the inequality that emerged in society under the federalists' view of equal rights. "Thus in so far as the equal rights are freely exercised, they are bound to result in inequalities; and these inequalities are bound to make for their own perpetuation."[27]

Over time this difference has come to be seen in terms of negative versus positive rights. Negative rights are things one already possesses, and the government cannot, or at least should not, take away. Again, these are summed up in the Bill of Rights protections of rights such as free speech and religion. Positive rights are things you do not have innately and that, when absent, the government should provide, such as food and a job.

There is an inherent conflict between the two. Exercising negative rights does not require anything from anyone else. One can speak, but no one needs to listen. Positive rights, when lacking, cannot be obtained except by placing a burden on others. One may have a right to food or shelter, but someone else must provide what is lacking. This is called charity if it is done voluntarily. It requires force if the government does it. This conflict did not go unnoticed by the progressives as Croly pointed out,

> The Constitution was the expression not only of a political faith, but also of political fears. It was wrought both as the organ of the national interest and as the bulwark of certain individual and local rights. The Federalists sought to surround private property, freedom of contract, and personal liberty with an impregnable legal fortress; and they were forced by their opponents to amend the original draft of the Constitution in order to include a still more stringent bill of individual and state rights.[28]

Thus, he predicted that,

27   H. Croly, "The Promise of American Life," 11 1909. [Online]. Available: https://www.gutenberg.org/files/14422/14422-h/14422-h.htm. [Accessed 8 10 2020]
28   H. Croly, "The Promise of American Life," 11 1909. [Online]. Available: https://www.gutenberg.org/files/14422/14422-h/14422-h.htm. [Accessed 8 10 2020]

> The time may come when the fulfillment of a justifiable democratic purpose may demand the limitation of certain rights, to which the Constitution affords such absolute guarantees;[29]

The federalists' view of rights emerged from the enlightenment view of the individual. The rights in the Bill of Rights have that focus. The intellectual background of progressives as it developed over the nineteenth century focused more on equality and thus the group. This different focus on individual rights vs. group equality came to define the two movements and is the root of much of the modern political disagreement. This disagreement stems from the fact that while both are desirable, liberty and equality are mutually exclusive. The more you have of one, the less you will have of the other.

Process Versus Results

The different perspectives on these fundamental issues result in very different approaches to many questions. In particular, over the issue of process versus results. In many ways, this is a glass half-empty or half-full question. Both the federalists and the progressives would agree that both are important. Both groups desire to have good processes that produce good results. But, like liberty and equality, what happens when they conflict?

For example, consider a court trial. Which is more important, that the rules of the court be followed or that justice is done? Again we all would want both. But what about when following the rules leads to injustice with the guilty going free or the innocent convicted? When the innocent are convicted, there is some ability for correction, but what about when the guilty go free?

Federalists and progressives frequently divide on this question. Concerns about government structure with carefully constructed checks and balances are essentially issues of process. As we saw above, Progressives see these as getting in the way of the results

29   H. Croly, "The Promise of American Life," 11 1909. [Online]. Available: https://www.gutenberg.org/files/14422/14422-h/14422-h.htm. [Accessed 8 10 2020]

they seek. Likewise, progressive concerns about inequalities, either political, social, or economic, focus on results. So on this question, federalists tilt toward the process, progressives toward results. This difference could be seen in the arguments around the Presidential election dispute in 2000, which was a very close election where the outcome depended on recounts in Florida. One side argued you could not change the rules after the election (process), while the other argued for counting every vote (result).

It is not that progressives don't care about process or federalists about results. It is a question over which is more important. Where does each group focus? In many cases, the correct answer is not at all clear. For example, in court, one might be tempted to argue that justice is more important than the rules. But if you start ignoring the rules in favor of justice, do you still have justice? Given the rules are there to help find justice, how would you know? This is a difference that would grow over time to become a major division today.

A Series of Changes

These fundamental differences led the early progressives to enact a series of major changes to the government. In 1913 the 16th amendment was ratified, permitting an income tax. This amendment was followed a few months later by the 17th amendment allowing for the direct election of U.S. Senators. The 17th Amendment somewhat weakened one of the checks and balances, particularly the dual sovereignty of the state and federal government. Until that point, the primary role of the Senate had been to represent the states, particularly the state governments, which elected them. 1919 saw the 18th amendment ushering in Prohibition while the 19th amendment expanded the vote to women.

While supported by many people for a variety of reasons, these four amendments were important for progressives. Their efforts to create a better society required a larger, more centralized government to ensure uniformity and economic rights. A large government required a better source of revenue, one the income tax provides.

The other three amendments represented the progressive ideals of weakening checks and balances (17th), perfecting society to perfect humanity(18th), and expanding direct democracy(19th).

Progressives, however, were not completely dominant, and there was some pushback, particularly after Wilson's Presidency and WWI. Calvin Coolidge, in a speech on the 150th anniversary of the Declaration of Independence, said,

The 19th Amendment

> It is not so much then for the purpose of undertaking to proclaim new theories and principles that this annual celebration is maintained, but rather to reaffirm and reestablish those old theories and principles which time and the unerring logic of events have demonstrated to be sound.[30]

On the one hand, this is just a nice speech on the Declaration. Yet, in the context of the period, Coolidge was arguing against the progressives' new way of approaching the government based on new "theories and principles." He went on to argue that rather than moving forward, progressives were taking us backward.

> About the Declaration there is a finality that is exceedingly restful. It is often asserted that the world has made a great deal of progress since 1776, that we have had new thoughts and new experiences which have given us a great advance over the people of that day, and that we may therefore very well discard their conclusions for something more modern. But that reasoning cannot be applied to this great charter. If all men are created equal, that is final. If they are endowed with inalienable rights, that is final. If governments derive

30   C. Coolidge, "The Inspiration of the Declaration," 5 7 1926. [Online]. Available: https://constitution.hillsdale.edu/document.doc?id=217. [Accessed 8 10 2020]

their just powers from the consent of the governed, that is final. No advance, no progress can be made beyond these propositions. If anyone wishes to deny their truth or their soundness, the only direction in which he can proceed historically is not forward, but backward toward the time when there was no equality, no rights of the individual, no rule of the people. Those who wish to proceed in that direction cannot lay claim to progress. They are reactionary. Their ideas are not more modern, but more ancient, than those of the Revolutionary fathers.[31]

Calvin Coolidge

Following Coolidge, Herbert Hoover, another progressive, became president. His two appointments to the Supreme Court shifted the Court towards the progressive view.

In particular, Justice Owen Roberts became the swing vote for many progressive decisions. O'Gorman and & Young sold policies for Hartford Fire Insurance Company. New Jersey law required commissions to be "reasonable." O'Gorman thought 25 percent was reasonable. Hartford disagreed and only paid twenty. The lower court sided with Hartford and ruled 25 percent was unreasonable. O'Gorman and & Young appealed to the Supreme Court claiming the New Jersey Law was unconstitutional because it deprived them of property without the due process of law, the property in question being the five percent difference in the rates of commission.

Prior to Justice Roberts joining the court, the Supreme Court was split 4-4, meaning the lower court ruling would stand without any real settlement of the issues at stake. It was reargued when

31   C. Coolidge, "The Inspiration of the Declaration," 5 7 1926. [Online]. Available: https://constitution.hillsdale.edu/document.doc?id=217. [Accessed 8 10 2020]

Justice Roberts joined, and he became the fifth vote in this key ruling. O'Gorman still lost, and once again, the ruling is more important than the decision. Justice Louis Brandeis, writing for the justices in the majority, said that states could require that rates be "reasonable." More importantly, Brandeis argued that the Court must presume laws are Constitutional unless there were clear facts to the contrary. The dissenting justices argue the burden should be on the government to show a law was needed.

With many issues, including issues of law, there are not just two sides. For example, while something could be clearly right or clearly wrong, often, there is a gray area in between where things are not so clear. When this happens, the question becomes who gets the benefit from any doubt? Brandeis' new rule was significant because it meant the government, not the citizen, benefits from any doubt.

In *Nebbia v. New York* (1934), this presumption of constitutionality was again used to uphold a New York law establishing milk prices. Leo Nebbia offered his customer a free loaf of bread if they purchased two quarts of milk at the price established by New York law. Again, the question was to what extent the government could control commerce. Can the government do what it wants, or must it have a good reason for the laws they enact?

This case highlights an important issue in such a decision. Judges rule on the evidence and arguments for and against presented to them, looking at the Constitution, the law, and the legislative history. As such, this is not asking if a good case might be made. The question here is whether the Government needs to make such a case in the first place. More importantly, where there is doubt, who gets the benefit of that doubt, the citizen or the government? Under the new standard, the government gets the benefit of the doubt. Nebbia was convicted of violating the law and fined. He appealed to the Supreme Court and lost.

The Great Depression and the resultant election of Franklin Roosevelt provided the next big opportunity for progressives. The 20th amendment (1933) shortened the time between the election and inauguration. The 21st amendment (1933) repealed the 18th, as Prohibition was considered, by then, a failure. Still, the real change made by progressives in this era was in the realms of reinterpreting the Constitution rather than amending it.

A major aspect of this was the continuing transformation of the presidency begun under Theodore Roosevelt. The federalists saw Congress as the most important branch of government. The President, described in Article II, could only execute the laws passed by Congress. Progressives wanted a stronger national government freed from checks and balances, led by a stronger President. Wilson argued concerning the office several years before entering it,

Franklin Delano Roosevelt

> for he is also the political leader of the nation, or has it in his choice to be. The nation as a whole has chosen him, and is conscious that it has no other political spokesman in affairs. His is the only national voice in affairs. Let him once win the admiration and confidence of the country, and no other single force can withstand him, no combination of forces will easily overpower him... The President is at Liberty, both in law and conscience, to be as big a man as he can. His capacity will set the limit; and if Congress be overborne by him, it will be no fault of the makers of the Constitution.[32]

From the progressives, we get our modern notions of the President with a legislative agenda and mandates, largely reversing the President and Congress's importance from that of the federal-

---

32 W. Wilson, "Constitutional Government of the United States," 1908. [Online]. Available: https://archive.org/details/constitutionalgo00wils/page/70/mode/2up. [Accessed 8 10 2020], pp 69-70

ists. Building on the progressive foundations laid by Theodore Roosevelt and Wilson, Franklin Roosevelt transformed our concept of the federal government. Before, the federal government was largely restricted to interstate issues and foreign policy. Under Roosevelt, the federal government became deeply involved in many aspects of everyday life.

Believing in the rule of administrators, a major part of Roosevelt's New Deal was creating nearly 70 new federal agencies with a virtual alphabet soup of initials dealing with all sorts of problems. Given the Depression, not surprisingly, there were areas such as

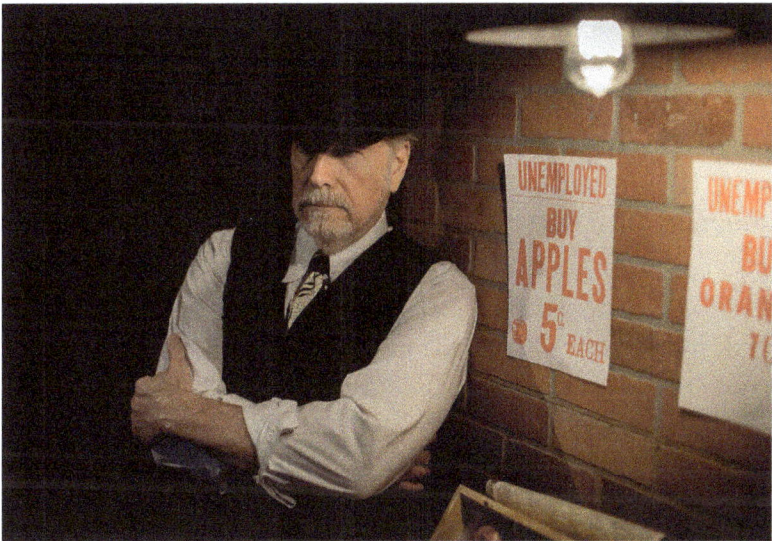

Surviving During the Great Depression

banking and agriculture. Still, progressives believe in transforming society to transform human nature, so things like the Federal Art Project (FPA) were also created. As these new agencies wrote a growing number of regulations, they effectively transferred some of the Legislative role to the Executive Branch. The agencies would write the regulation (legislative) and then see that they were followed (executive). Eventually, these agencies would take on part of the Judiciary's role in creating administrative courts. The trials in these courts determine if individuals and companies are guilty of violating the administrators' regulations; Legislative, Executive, and Judiciary roles all in one organization.

The New Deal was a massive change in how the federal government operated. Many New Deal laws and agencies soon ran into trouble in the Supreme Court and were ruled unconstitutional. Historian David B. Woolner, in his book, *The Last 100 Days: FDR at War and Peace*, wrote, "Over the next 13 months, the court struck down more pieces of legislation than at any other time in U.S. history."

A centerpiece of the New Deal was the National Recovery Administration (NRA) created in 1933. Among other things, this allowed businesses and unions to establish "Codes of Fair Competition." Once approved by the President, these codes had the force of law. This was too much even for the Supreme Court's progressives. In a unanimous opinion, the Court ruled the NRA unconstitutional, as it transferred the legislative power to the President.

A Progressive Court

During this period, the Court was pretty much balanced 4-4, with Justice Owen Roberts, a Hoover appointee, being the swing vote. In O'Gorman and Nebbia, Roberts sided with the progressives. At other times he didn't. The details are many and varied and still a matter of debate, but the broad outline is fairly clear. In the early years of FDR's presidency, many of his New Deal laws and agencies ran into problems with the courts.

In an example of results over process, Roosevelt tried to change the process to get the results he wanted. In 1937, he proposed expanding the number of justices on the Supreme Court. More justices would give him the ability to appoint judges favorable to his progressive plans and this became known as court packing. Even many in his own party criticized his plan and it failed.

Conventional history holds that in *West Coast Hotel v. Parrish* (1937), Justice Roberts changed his position and voted to uphold a minimum wage law. The previous year he had voted the opposite way on a similar case. The reason for the change was supposedly FDR's court-packing plan, announced shortly before the ruling. The claim is he changed his vote to take the pressure off of packing the Court. This has come down in history as the *switch in time that saved nine.*

Yet, the explanation appears to be false. Decisions in the Supreme Court are prepared long before the time they are announced. There must be time for a vote, and then all the decisions and dissents are written. In cases where multiple judges join an opinion, the opinion must be reviewed. In short, months often pass between the time of the vote and when the decision is announced. Records show that Judge Roberts voted to uphold the law months before FDR proposed packing the Court. The reason for his change from the previous case rests in legal differences between cases and not in FDR's attempt to pack the Supreme Court.

While Roosevelt's court-packing scheme failed, he did get a more progressive court because of retirements. Running for an unprecedented third and then a fourth term, he replaced all the justices with progressive justices by the end of his presidency. These judges with a progressive understanding of the Constitution greatly expanded the federal government's scope, far beyond what had been formerly understood by enumerated powers through a series of rulings.

For example, the Constitution gives as one of Congress's enumerated powers the power "To regulate Commerce with foreign Nations, and among the several States, and with the Indian Tribes." In NLRB versus Jones & Laughlin Steel Corp.(1937), the plaintiff argued that the NLRB (National Labor Relations Board), created in 1935, was going beyond the regulation of interstate commerce and infringing on "local concerns." In their decision, the Court allowed the federal government to control not just interstate commerce, but also local commerce which has "such a close and substantial relation to interstate commerce that their control is essential or appropriate to protect that commerce from burden and obstruction."

The Constitution limited the Congress to controlling interstate commerce, but here the definition of interstate commerce was being greatly expanded to include pretty much anything that could in any way be linked to interstate commerce. In *United States v. Darby* (1941), the Court ruled the federal government could regulate "intrastate activities where they have a substantial effect on interstate commerce." Note the use of the word 'activities' as these need not themselves be commerce. *Wickard v. Filburn* (1942) arose because the Agricultural Adjustment Act, passed in 1933, limited what a farmer could grow. Roscoe Filburn grew more than the quota allowed, but for private use, selling only what the quota allowed. The Court ruled that the government could limit his crops grown for private use.

By the end of his term, the progressive nature of Roosevelt's plan was clear in his annual message to Congress in 1944,

> As our nation has grown in size and stature, however— as our industrial economy expanded—these political rights proved inadequate to assure us equality in the pursuit of happiness. We have come to a clear realization of the fact that true individual freedom cannot exist without economic security and independence. "Necessitous men are not free men." People who are hungry and out of a job are the stuff of which dictatorships are made. In our day these economic truths have become accepted as self-evident. We have accepted, so to speak, a second Bill of Rights under which a new basis of security and prosperity can be established for all—regardless of station, race, or creed.

Franklin Roosevelt was the only president to break the tradition set by Washington of only serving two terms. Following his death, the 22nd amendment was passed to ensure that it would never happen again.

In the 1950s, the issue of segregation made its way to the courts again, this time over schools. While extremely controversial at the time, today, few question the correctness of the ruling in

68

Brown v. Board of Education (1954) or the lesser know but simultaneous ruling, *Bolling v. Sharpe* (1954). Both cases questioned the constitutionality of segregated schools. *Brown* for schools in Kansas, South Carolina, Virginia, and Delaware; *Bolling* concerned the District of Columbia. The Court ruled segregated schools unconstitutional based on the 14th amendment's equal protection clause in *Brown* and the 5th amendment Due Process clause in *Bolling*.

While few would question the ruling's correctness, there is some controversy over the ruling's reasoning. If, for nothing else, the reasoning in the two cases is inconsistent. Accepting the reasoning in one seems to question the reasoning in the other. In addition, the Court went beyond the evidence presented in court, the law, and the Constitution and based part of its decision on social sciences research.

Thus for some, Brown becomes the prime example of why the courts should be free to understand the Constitution in light of the modern context. This view is of a Living Constitution, a view with clear progressive roots. Others argue there was no need to go beyond the Constitution. The same decision could have been reached on purely constitutional grounds, particularly if the Court had concluded *Plessy v. Ferguson*, the case that ruled separate but equal did not violate the Constitution, was wrongly decided, something they stopped short of doing in Brown. These different views of the Constitution would come to shape much of the political debate in the Country.

The Current Era: Division, Conflict, Uncertainty (1964-Present)

More Amendments

The 1960s saw another group of Constitutional amendments ratified. The founders were reluctant to place the new federal government in any state. Doing so would give that state an inordinate say in the government. It would be the only place all Senators and Representatives lived. This concern has been seen in many states with the importance of their capital city. Often small insignificant cities were chosen to avoid power concentrating in big cities. Yet before long, these capitals grew to become big cities.

The Constitution avoids this problem and provides a separate federal district, not exceeding ten square miles, as the government seat. The District residents now participate in presidential elections, with the passage of the 23rd amendment in 1961.

In the early 1960s, the Declaration's promise that all men are created equal remained unfulfilled as it has been in the 1860s. At the March on Washington, August 28, 1963, Dr. Martin Luther King Jr. delivered one of the most historic speeches in American history, his *I Have a Dream* speech. On the step of the Lincoln Memorial, King began by pointing out that the Emancipation Proclamation was signed by Lincoln 100 years earlier, "But one hundred years later, the Negro still is not free;" He went on,

> When the architects of our republic wrote the magnificent words of the Constitution and the Declaration of Independence, they were signing a promissory note to which every American was to fall heir. This note was the promise that all men, yes, black men as well as white men, would be guaranteed the unalienable rights of life, Liberty, and the pursuit of happiness.

It was a call for America to live up to the principles upon which the country was founded and helped spur the Civil Rights legislation of the decade.

Martin Luther King (Wirestock - stock.adobe.com)

Despite the 15th amendment, voting rights in the South continued to be a problem for Blacks. They were kept from voting by various means, such as requiring a poll tax to be paid to register to vote. For example, North Carolina had a poll tax but exempted all those eligible to vote before the ratification of the 15th amendment. The 24th amendment, ratified in 1964, prohibits making any tax as a condition for voting.

For the last 17 months of his Presidency, Woodrow Wilson was incapacitated by a stroke. All communication went through his wife. Along with that, the assassination of John F. Kennedy revealed some weakness in the Constitution's plans for succession. These were addressed in the 25th amendment ratified in 1967. Finally, the controversy surrounding the Vietnam War led to the ratification of the 26th amendment in 1971. This amendment dropped the voting age from 21 to 18, based on the argument that if you are old enough to serve in the military and die for your country, you should be old enough to vote.

As mentioned earlier, along with the Bill of Rights, two other structural amendments were submitted to the states by the first Congress, but both failed to be ratified. One would have fixed the number of people that a House member could represent at no more than 50,000. This amendment fell short of ratification by one state three times. Two new states were added, and more states voted to ratify the amendment, but it always fell short by one vote. Today it would have required over 6,500 representatives if it had been ratified, rather than the current 435.

The other amendment required any congressional pay increase to take effect only after an election. This amendment also failed to be ratified. Unlike the more recent amendments, these amendments did not include a time limit. In 1982, Gregory Watson submitted a paper for his American Government class, arguing the amendment concerning congressional pay increases could, in theory, still be ratified. He got a C on the paper because the idea was considered too "far-fetched."

Gregory was not pleased, so he set out to prove he was right. He worked hard and got Maine to ratify the amendment in April 1983. On May 18, 1992, ratification by the required 38 states was complete. Watson then proceeded to apply for a grade change and was successful. Watson's teacher changed his grade to an A. Thus, when this book was written, the last amendment to the Constitution, the 27th, was also one of the first to be submitted to the states.

The ten years following the assassination of John F. Kennedy was, by any measure, a time of change, turmoil, and unrest. It also saw significant changes to progressivism, now generally called Liberalism, and the emergence of what would become the major federalist alternative view, Conservatism.

Major changes to progressivism were seen in the "Great Society" of the presidency of Lyndon Johnson, further expanding the role, purpose, and size of the federal government from the New Deal. In his Great Society speech, Johnson said, "The Great Society rests on abundance and Liberty for all. It demands an end to poverty and racial injustice." He went on to outline "three places where we begin to build the Great Society -- in our cities, in our countryside, and in our classrooms."

The concern in these areas was not new or unique to the Great Society. What was new was that these were to be concerns of the federal government, even beyond the expanded scope of governmental powers found in the New Deal.

> The Great Society is a place where every child can find knowledge to enrich his mind and to enlarge his talents. It is a place where leisure is a welcome chance to build and reflect, not a feared cause of boredom and restlessness. It is a place where the city of man serves not only the needs of the body and the demands of commerce but the desire for beauty and the hunger for community.

However laudable these goals may be, any government capable of carrying out such goals would be vastly larger and more powerful than anything envisioned by the federalists. The New Deal had been concerned with people who lacked food or a good job. Here, Johnson called for the government to meet the "desire for beauty and the hunger for community." The language referring to the "city of man" harkens back to St Augustine and his major work, the city of God, which contrasted the city of God (heaven) with the city of man (earth). For LBJ, the Great Society is a place where man can renew contact with nature. It is a place which honors creation for its own sake and for what it adds to the understanding of the race. It is a place where men are more concerned with the quality of their goals than the quantity of their goods.

In a speech at Howard University, Johnson again went beyond even the New Deal to argue,

Freedom is not enough... We seek not just freedom but opportunity. We seek not just legal equity but human ability, not just equality as a right and a theory but equality as a fact and equality as a result.

Different Views of the Court

Lyndon B. Johnson

The most significant change in terms of the Constitution in this era was the growing importance of the Supreme Court. As discussed earlier, the federalists saw the courts as the weakest and least threatening of the three branches. Three factors came to change that. The first was the history of the court rulings on the Constitution. They were seen as the final arbitrator when it came to the Constitution. The courts' role was respected, even with what are now clearly seen as bad decisions, such as *Dred Scott* and *Plessy v. Ferguson*.

A second major change was the Court's move beyond a strict reliance on the Constitution to include other factors such as social sciences, as in *Brown v. Board of Education*. Finally, the Court's progressive dominance that came out of FDR's presidency resulted in an expansive view of government duties and rights, one in stark contrast with the federalists' limited view of government.

As a result, in the decades following 1960, these two distinct views of the Constitution and the Court's role in interpreting it came into conflict. One is the Living Constitution, the ideal going back to Wilson, who described the government as a living

74

thing. Wilson said, "the courts are the instruments of the nation's growth." He went on to argue about the Supreme Court,

> But it is true that their power is political; that if they had interpreted the Constitution in its strict letter, as some proposed, and not in its spirit, like the charter of a business corporation and not like the charter of a living government, the vehicle of a nation's life, it would have proved a strait-jacket, a means not of Liberty and development, but of mere restriction and embarrassment.

The Court needed to be free to understand the Constitution in light of the changing circumstances of an ever-changing and growing society, a progressive society. Unfortunately, this meant the Court was seen as increasingly political. While ideology, not politics, drove their decisions, the result was they were making decisions that in previous decades had been left to the legislative body. At a minimum, they were making decisions that until then had been political and thus seemed political.

While some always defended the federalists and the original understanding of the Constitution, this formalized into a competing view called Originalism. As the name implies, originalism holds that the Constitution should be understood as it was originally written. There is an amendment process if the document is inadequate or needs updating, which has been done 27 times.

Nothing shows the increasing polarization between these two views more than the politicization of judicial appointments, particularly the Supreme Court. Even into the 1980s, the appointments to the Supreme Court were minor stories. Antonin Scalia, appointed by Ronald Reagan to the Supreme Court in 1986, faced no real opposition during his senate hearing and was approved 98-0.

The first real fight occurred the following year when Ronald Reagan appointed Robert Bork. His appointment sparked the first in what would become a series of hotly contested nomination fights. Bork was defeated, and Anthony Kennedy went on the Court instead. The reason for the battle was simple; these two views of the Constitution produce starkly different rulings. If the federalists' view of the courts as the weakest and least important branch was no longer valid and judges were to take on a larger role in determining public policy, then who the judge is matters a great deal.

The Supreme Court under the progressives had taken on this new role since the mid-1930s. As the number of Originalists on the Supreme Court grew, replacing judges with a Living Constitution view, the battles started and have continued to this day. Originalists and Living Constitutionalists have been roughly equally divided for the last several decades, with one or more justices being swing votes. In 2018, Anthony Kennedy, then the swing vote, retired, resulting in one of the largest fights. In the end, Brett Kavanaugh was confirmed, giving Originalists a 5-4 majority. However, there was some question that Chief Justice Robert was becoming the new swing vote. Two years later, the Originalist majority expanded to 6-3 with the death of Ruth Bader Ginsburg and the appointment of Amy Coney Barrett. Kavanaugh and Barrett's appointments gave the federalists their first majority on the Supreme Court in 90 years.

Space does not permit discussing the wide range of cases or policy areas where the Court has become the determining factor; they span most aspects of life. Still, one case is a focal point for both sides, the prime example of either the need for an Originalist view or a Living Constitution, depending on which side you are on.

Roe v. Wade

Contrary to the common notion, *Roe* did not make abortion legal. Before *Roe*, abortion was a state issue, and as such, states were free to do what the people of that state wanted. From the founding of the country till 1967, abortion was largely illegal across the country. Initially this was based on common law, which restricted abortion after quickening, the time when the mother begins to feel the baby move. During the nineteenth century, many states passed specific laws limiting abortion. While before 1967, abortion was illegal across the country. Between 1967 and the Court's ruling, about a third of the states enacted laws to legalize abortion in at least some cases.

What *Roe* did was rule laws against abortion unconstitutional. It removed from states, and thus the people in those states, most of the ability to regulate abortion. As a matter of law, *Planned Parenthood v. Casey* (1992) was the major case on abortion before *Dobbs*, as it significantly changed the standards set in *Roe*. Still, *Roe* remains the symbol for both sides.

Roe is a good example because the Court's decision is perfectly in line with the Living Constitution view and, in fact, requires it. It is also a perfect example of the Court taking on a legislative role from the Originalists' perspective. The Founding Fathers certainly could have included a right to abortion if they had wanted. After all, abortion is not a new technology like TV or computers, which would have been unfamiliar. Abortion was around a long time before the Constitution was written, but it is not mentioned. Because of dual Sovereignty with the states, since it is not mentioned, from an Originalist point of view, the Court would have to rule this is not an issue for the federal courts. It was an issue of customary law and, like laws with murder or contracts, left to the people to decide through their state governments.

The Court based its ruling in *Roe* on an earlier ruling in *Griswold v. Connecticut* (1965), which similarly found another right, in this case, the right to privacy. In the ruling on Griswold, Justice Douglas went beyond the Constitution's plain text to justify a right to privacy. He said the right to privacy was to be found in "penumbras, formed by emanations from those guarantees that help give them life and substance."

If this talk of penumbras and emanations sounds vague, it is. Penumbras come from the Latin words meaning 'almost' and 'shadow.' It refers, for example, to the area visible around the sun only during an eclipse. Douglas argued the rights specified in the Constitution give off "emanations." These emanations create shadows where he and the other judges in the majority discovered some rights not specified by the Constitution's framers. They made these constitutional rights, in this case, a right to privacy.

Once the Court discovered these new rights, they became precedent for future judges to use in future rulings. Originalists argue that such legal reasoning could be used to justify pretty much anything a judge would like to find. It turns the Constitution into a legal Rorschach test where judges are pretty much free to see what they want to see.

As the Constitution did not address abortion, the Court could not base its ruling on what it said when *Roe* came along. The Court, using the reasoning from Griswold, was able to discover the right to abortion. This reasoning is perfectly valid from a Living Constitutional view. From an Originalist view, *Roe* is something imposed on the Constitution, not something derived from it. Thus, polarization.

What-is vs. Should-be

What makes the issue of the courts' ideology so difficult is that much of the battle takes place over the results rather than the reasoning. In this case, the issue of abortion itself, rather than what is the Constitutional view of abortion. If, as you have read this, you agreed with *Roe* or disagreed with *Roe* because of your views on abortion, you have fallen victim to the very problem of the ruling versus the reasoning.

There is also a problem in that the differing views use different types of reasoning, what-is and should-be. What-is reasoning focuses on the very narrow issue of what the law is on a given issue. Using what-is reasoning, one can look at the statutes to determine the speed limit on a given road at a given time. Thus, it is perfectly possible to determine that the law said the speed limit was 25 but

78

believe that it should have been different. This is because what-is reasoning is only concerned with what the law is on a given issue.

Should-be reasoning, in many respects, is the opposite. Rather than focus on what the law says, should-be reasoning attempts to determine what the law should be. This type of reasoning leads to a much broader range of concerns. For a speed limit on a given road, you might look at issues like traffic, the neighborhood, visibility, and the number of curves.

When it comes to Originalist vs. Living Constitutional views, Originalist confines themselves to what-is reasoning, or at least that is the goal. The key difference with the Living Constitution is that should-be concerns do play a role to some degree. If it is the role of the Judge to interpret the Constitution in light of the ever-changing society, the fundamental question changes from what does the Constitution say to become what should our understanding of the Constitution be given these changes?

These two different views of the Constitution have served as the backdrop for the abortion debates for the last 50 years. Each side made arguments that resulted in more conflict than anything else because these arguments were working in different frameworks. For Pro-Life supporters to say that abortion is not mentioned in the Constitution is a what-is argument. For Pro-Choice supporters to say that women need access to abortion is a should-be argument. Both sides were making legitimate arguments from their perspective.

In contrast, the other side's arguments were, at least to some degree, irrelevant. From a Living Constitution point of view, the fact that the Constitution does not mention abortion is not all that important given the evolving standards of the time. From an Originalist point of view, should-be arguments are for the legislature, not the courts. Both sides were talking past each other, so the controversy continued.

With a new originalist majority on the Supreme Court, it was not long before an abortion case came before the Court, which happened in 2021 with *Dobbs v. Jackson Women's Health Organization*. At issue was a Mississippi law that prohibited abortion after the fifteenth week, except in cases of "medical emergency or the case of severe fetal abnormality." The issue before the court was whether the state of Mississippi was allowed to pass and enforce such a law.

While not a complete abortion ban, this law directly conflicted with the standards set out in both *Roe* and the subsequent and controlling *Casey* decisions. Both sides agreed that allowing the law would overrule these decisions either formally or informally, as *Brown v. Board of Education* had effectively overruled *Plessy v. Ferguson* without actually doing so.

The majority decision by Justice Alito was a very solid originalist decision. As he wrote, *Roe* was an "abuse of judicial authority," which was true from an originalist point of view. He described the reasoning in *Roe* as "remarkably loose in its treatment of the constitutional text." As for the historical analysis upon which *Roe* was based, that

> ranged from the constitutionally irrelevant (e.g., its discussion of abortion in antiquity) to the plainly incorrect (e.g., its assertion that abortion was probably never a crime under the common law). After cataloging a wealth of other information having no bearing on the meaning of the Constitution, the opinion concluded with a numbered set of rules much like those that might be found in a statute enacted by a legislature.

It should not be hard to see the originalist foundation upon which Alito's arguments are based. He went on to say,

> *Roe* was egregiously wrong from the start. Its reasoning was exceptionally weak, and the decision had damaging consequences. And far from bringing about a national settlement of the abortion issue, *Roe* and *Casey* have enflamed debate and deepened division.

Alito's decision lays out the reason and justifications for his claim. It should be noted that many supporters of abortion have expressed a similar view, and Alito cites a number of them in his decision. Yet, from a Living Constitutional perspective, these arguments, while possibly valid, are not all that important. For them, Abortion should be a right, and thus *Roe* and *Casey* were good decisions.

The final argument used to defend *Roe* and *Casey* is *stare decisis*, the legal term describing the respect given for prior decisions. The general idea is that *Roe* and *Casey* were settled laws and should not be overturned. This is not a blanket rule. If it were, P*lessy v. Ferguson*, with its view of separate but equal, would still be the Constitutional view. Many Constitutional rulings overturn, in whole or in part, earlier precedent. In fact, *Casey* overruled many of the provisions in *Roe*, which is why it was the controlling decision, not *Roe*. As for the length of time, *Plessy* was in force longer than *Roe* and *Casey* combined.

The question was not could *Dobbs* overturn *Roe* and *Casey*, but should it? Alito spends considerable time going through the court's history and reasoning on *stare decisis*. He summed this up as follows,

> five factors weigh strongly in favor of overruling *Roe* and *Casey*: the nature of their error, the quality of their reasoning, the "workability" of the rules they imposed on the country, their disruptive effect on other areas of the law, and the absence of concrete reliance.

The last reason refers to how much overturning *Roe* and *Casey* would disturb those things that require advanced planning. Alito spends many pages laying out his arguments for each of the five reasons. In the end, the court ruled,

> We end this opinion where we began. Abortion presents a profound moral question. The Constitution does not prohibit the citizens of each State from regulating or prohibiting abortion. *Roe* and *Casey* arrogated that authority. We now overrule those decisions and return

that authority to the people and their elected representatives.

A Political Decision?

Many were upset by this decision, claiming it was political. As I argued above, decisions based on Living Constitutional views were not political, and neither was this. *Dobbs* is a carefully reasoned and very legitimate decision from the originalist perspective. It is not a Pro-Life decision.

A Pro-Life decision would have looked at the historical record that abortion was generally illegal until the latter part of the Twentieth century, and given the advancement in medical knowledge and technology that allows us to see babies in the womb, conclude that a fetus is a person deserving the protection of the law afforded to all other persons. In short, they would have ruled abortion illegal in some or all cases.

Yet the *Dobbs* decision does not do that. Instead, it said abortion was not a Constitutional issue, thereby "returning that authority to the people and their elected represen-tatives." States with large Pro-Choice majorities will see little if any change. States with large Pro-Life Majorities will see strong limits on

The Supreme Court Building with Security

abortion. States with populations in between will see some limits, but not bans, reflecting the views of their population.

Those who want a total abortion ban will not like that some states still permit it. Those who want no restrictions on abortion will not like that some states have restrictions. Neither side will get everything they want, and laws will vary from state to state, as they do on various other issues. As Winston Churchill famously said,

> Many forms of Government have been tried, and will be tried in this world of sin and woe. No one pretends that democracy is perfect or all-wise. Indeed it has been said that democracy is the worst form of Government except for all those other forms that have been tried from time to time....

The Future

Today the country is more polarized than at any time since the 1860s. Behind the slavery issue that drove the Civil War were the different views of the Declaration of Independence and the Constitution represented by John C. Calhoun, who saw in them a great error on the one side, and Abraham Lincoln, who saw them as central to our understanding of the country . Today's polarization is similarly driven by different views of these documents. The federalists believe that these documents and principles are eternal and should be preserved and followed. They are as valid today as when they were written nearly 250 years ago.

The progressives' view holds that while these documents were appropriate for their time, society at the beginning of the 20th century was different from the beginning of the 19th century, just as the beginning of the 21st century is different from the 20th. These different times call for different views of the Constitution, a living view that changes to keep up with the times.

These are mutually exclusive views. The federalists believed human nature was fixed; progressives believe society's problems cause human nature's problems. It is the role of the government to perfect human nature. The federalists wanted a government close to the people, with state and local governments being the most important. The federal government should play a limited and carefully defined role. The progressives want a stronger, more centralized government to manage all aspects of people's lives, even beauty.

The federalists wanted a government based on liberty. The government's role was to protect liberty from those who would impinge on those freedoms. The progressives wanted equality, initially of access, and then later increasingly in the outcome. The federalists focused on the individual; the progressives on the group. The federalists wanted a system of checks and balances; the progressives wanted a government that could get things done. The federalists wanted power vested in the people or their duly elected representatives. The progressives wanted some aspects of government separated from politics and managed by dispassionate administrators.

Behind many of the most difficult issues we face today are these divisions and disagreements over how to proceed. It is not, as it is often presented, simply a matter of political bickering among the parties. 'If they would just put politics aside,' the claim goes, 'they could solve some of the problems facing the country.' Such thinking ignores there are serious and fundamental differences on how to proceed. Even when there is general agreement over a problem, these fundamental differences lead to very different and incompatible solutions.

For example, Progressives think the federal government should be expanded to ensure equality. The Federalists believe the government is already too large such that it threatens liberty. What is the middle ground between larger and smaller? There is none.

Though many of the details are different, we are at a point similar to that faced by the country when Lincoln gave his House Divide speech. To paraphrase Lincoln,

A house divided against itself cannot stand. This government cannot endure, permanently half federalist and half progressive.

At some point, a choice will be made. The country can go one way, or the other. The real question is, will this be a conscious choice made by the people after careful and thoughtful deliberation? Or will this decision be made by drifting into one side or the other, as a secondary result of elections fought on other issues?

There is a third option. Like the delegates at the convention, the country could discuss and debate the various options and work out a compromise. As with the convention, such a debate will not be quick or easy. Like the convention, it will probably at times be contentious. Neither side will get everything they want, but again that is the nature of compromise. This path seems to have worked out pretty well the first time.

When leaving the Constitutional Convention, Benjamin Franklin was supposedly asked what type of government had they given us? He is supposed to have replied, "A republic, if you can keep it." The question today is, do we want to?

www.ingramcontent.com/pod-product-compliance
Lightning Source LLC
Chambersburg PA
CBHW071139280326

41935CB00010B/1296